OYSTERS

OYSTERS

RECIPES *that* BRING HOME *a* TASTE *of the* SEA

CYNTHIA NIMS

Photography by Jim Henkens

SASQUATCH BOOKS
SEATTLE

THIS BOOK IS DEDICATED to all those—friends and family, chefs and farmers, writers and advocates—who keep me inspired in this wonderful world of food

Printed in China

Published by Sasquatch Books

20 19 18 17 16   9 8 7 6 5 4 3 2 1

Editor: Gary Luke
Production editor: Em Gale
Photographs: Jim Henkens
Design: Joyce Hwang
Copyeditor: Michelle
Hope Anderson

Library of Congress Cataloging-
in-Publication Data is available.

ISBN: 978-1-63217-037-8

Sasquatch Books
1904 Third Avenue, Suite 710
Seattle, WA 98101
(206) 467-4300
www.sasquatchbooks.com
custserv@sasquatchbooks.com

CONTENTS

WHAT IS IT ABOUT OYSTERS?

They inspire hip oyster bars, backyard grilling feasts, and elegant cele-bration meals. They evoke songs, poems, and fashion shows. They bring out our competitive streak to see who can shuck and slurp the most. They prompt pilgrimages to their home territory, which might include late-night forays to moonlit bays seeking the best of the season at its pinnacle of freshness. They satisfy our hunger, fuel our romance, and feed our souls. I've written quite a lot about Northwest foods over the years, and no other food seems to strike the kind of food-culture chord that oysters do.

Oyster culture is a natural part of our lives all along the Pacific Coast of the United States and Canada. Both culture in terms of the customs and values of us who live here and the practical business of raising oys-ters in this prolific growing environment. For some it's a particularly rich dose of both types of culture, as many oyster-growing operations are now run by third, fourth, even fifth generations of family members keeping their slice of local oyster heritage alive.

The sheer volume of production reflects the geography of this coast, with its countless bays, sounds, inlets, channels, and coves that provide ideal habitats for oysters. And the quality of those oysters is a direct product of the water they live in, nutrient rich and managed in ways to help preserve healthy seafood populations. The diversity of flavors that Pacific Coast oysters have echoes variants in the types of phytoplankton, zooplankton, and other microorganisms that thrive in the region's water, not to mention variations in water depth, temperature, tidal activity, and other environmental attributes.

This conglomeration of natural influences on the oyster's character has come to be known as *meroir*, the seaworthy version of terroir. We on the Pacific Coast are lucky to live in a place where the meroir produces superlative oysters that folks just can't seem to get enough of.

Oysters have a capacity to transport us, right there in our kitchen or on our oyster-bar stool, more than other foods. When we hold the creature in its pure form, it only takes a short leap of the imagination to put us on the shore where it was harvested. The fact that the shell may carry along some evidence of its marine cohorts makes it seem all the more vivid: barnacles, a tuft of seaweed, maybe a minuscule oyster or mussel. And that liquor that surrounds the oyster in its shell—it seems pure essence of the sea, a taste of place like none other.

I realize that not everyone is mad about oysters, nor necessarily feels transported when consuming them. But I will say that the mere mention of this book's topic launched more interesting conversations with both friends and strangers than I recall from any other project.

There was my weekend on Washington's Long Beach Peninsula, at the historic Shelburne Inn. I've known the owners, David Campiche and Laurie Anderson, for many years, originally in the context of doing wild mushroom research. On this recent early winter visit, I'd been to see Goose Point and Ekone oyster operations on Willapa Bay en route to teaching a wild mushroom class at the inn. As David put down a plate of his Hangtown fry (eggs cooked frittata style with oysters and bacon; he adds spinach and a dash of Parmesan) the next morning, he talked about growing up in that area. And how his Ilwaco High School football team was hard to beat because some of them worked at collecting oysters on the Willapa Bay mud flats, building up extraordinarily strong thigh muscles with each bushel they filled.

Another time I had just flown into San Francisco International Airport and was picking up my rental car. The fellow at the counter, being friendly while taking care of the paperwork, asked where I was headed. "Up to Tomales Bay," I said, "to have some oysters at Hog Island." "You know how I like to cook oysters?" he offered, without any prompting from me. "Just put them right on the grill and cook them until they pop open. Some Tabasco sauce. That's it." I nodded in total agreement. "Oh, and Hennessy Cognac, that's what I drink with those oysters." Hmm, now that was a pairing idea I hadn't considered before.

The road trips I took while researching this book amplified my realization that oysters are the source of hallmark Pacific Coast experiences. Oyster lovers can visit oyster farms, buy from the source, slurp oysters on the beach, enjoy a picnic within view of the oyster beds, and attend myriad oyster-centric events. There are many dynamic traditions built around oysters that exemplify the region's oyster engagement.

I cut my journalistic teeth on the subject of seafood as an editor at *Simply Seafood* magazine, published by a Seattle company founded by former fishermen who put out a couple of publications for the seafood industry as well. That magazine position was my first job back home after my culinary education in France. It was there that I wrote a 1997 article about the then renaissance of oyster bars. And it was thanks to that job that I found myself one chilly, dank late-fall morning on the doorstep of Julia Child's home in Cambridge, Massachusetts.

It's not as though she didn't know I was coming and wouldn't have let me in otherwise. But showing up with a cooler containing Olympia oysters and some first-of-the-season Dungeness crab in hand seemed to have swiftened my entry. Within moments I was in her warm kitchen and she shucked open an oyster, slurping it down with glee. That was just one of many occasions that have made clear to me how broad and devoted the fan base is for oysters from the Pacific Coast.

When it comes to exploring oysters, there are interesting parallels drawn to the world of wine. As we sip different wines from different places, sometimes side by side, it helps us better understand the range of options available as we form opinions about what suits our personal palate best. The same is true of sampling oysters, particularly when various types can be tasted at the same time for a clear comparison. This is the best way to appreciate how much diversity of flavor there is to be had with oysters. Soon you learn that not all oysters are the same, which invites only more delicious exploration.

Opportunities for just that kind of exploration abound along the Pacific Coast, fueled in large part by access to oysters through a number of channels. Beyond the usual retail store and restaurant options, some oyster farms sell direct to customers on-site, whether through a simple service window or in a small store with other oyster-friendly offerings. A few oyster growers have gone so far as to open restaurants at which they showcase their product from the oyster bed direct to the customer's plate.

But oyster-farm-to-table dining isn't a new phenomenon here. The origin of today's Oregon Oyster Farms and Dan & Louis Oyster Bar can trace to a mid-nineteenth-century shipwreck off Yaquina Bay, which precipitated an unscheduled introduction to the vast supply of oysters found in the bay. Meinert Wachsmuth was on board and didn't stay in the area at the time but retired there later. His son Louis Charles Wachsmuth is the one who took the oyster and ran with it in the early twentieth century, raising oysters on the coast and serving oysters in Portland. The family no longer owns the oyster-growing business, but its legacy lives on in both establishments. It also lives on in chef Cory Schreiber, great-great-grandson of Meinert, longtime chef/owner of Portland's beloved (and now closed) Wildwood restaurant and today chef/instructor at the Art Institute of Portland. He visited the family oyster beds many times growing up and hung out in the shucking room where the radio blasted as women shucked and gossiped all day long. If not through genetics alone, his fate of an oyster-rich life was surely sealed with the baby shower in his honor held at the family oyster bar.

So you see that it is a rich fabric that's woven with oyster culture all along the Pacific Coast. Family traditions, commercial industry, celebrations, recreation, history, conversation, and pure culinary enjoyment can all be fed by the humble oyster.

BASICS

THE LIFE & TIMES OF THE MODERN OYSTER

HOW THEY GROW

What sets oysters apart from other creatures of the sea? As a mollusk, the oyster is related to a whole host of marine life, from abalone to octopus. Among those mollusks are shellfish—invertebrates with exoskeletons, or exterior skeletal structure—of which oysters fall in the class of bivalves. Like other bivalves, including clams, mussels, and scallops, an oyster is a filter feeder whose two (*bi*) hinged shells (*valves*) open to draw seawater across its gills, filtering out nutritious phytoplankton and other minute particles.

We easily see the differences in shape and size of the different bivalves. One characteristic you might not notice right off is that while most others have two identical shells, oysters have one cupped shell and one flat. They live differently too: clams burrow into the sand; mussels attach with byssal threads to rocks, piers, or other stationary objects; scallops propel themselves about and live more freely than the others. Oysters stay put; in the wild they content themselves with the spot where they landed on the beach, neither burrowing nor flitting around.

Given the static life they lead, the oysters' form of reproduction is far from intimate. Most oysters spew out sperm and eggs into the water, and the larvae that are produced swim around for a few weeks until they are large enough to consider settling down. However, Olympia oysters and European flat oysters are brooders. Males dispense sperm and females nab it to fertilize eggs held within their shells. The female will brood the larvae for about ten days, then spit them out to make their way in the world.

Regardless of how they came to be, oyster larvae float freely for a week or two, then seek out an anchor from which to grow. Their preferred new home will be another oyster shell, which explains the tiny hitchhiker oysters you may find on the surface of full-grown oysters you're about to shuck. That's one indication that your oyster was reared in an area with particularly ripe conditions for oyster spawning. (This also explains why some recreational oyster rules require the oysters be shucked on-site and the shells be left on the beach.) Once an oyster has settled on this new home, it is now an oyster spat. If it survives its juvenile years into adulthood, a Pacific oyster can live twenty years or more.

The biology of an oyster isn't just about the oyster. Oysters have an interesting and important role to play in the ecosystem they inhabit. Some consider them to be a "keystone species," one that has a disproportionately large impact on the environment in which they live and grow. Others use the term "ecosystem engineers," referencing the function they have in supporting and boosting resources for other sea life around them.

The majority of oysters harvested on the Pacific Coast are farm raised, the product of aquaculture. That notion, rightfully so, can raise red flags in our minds. What about the degradation of mangroves caused by shrimp farming in Southeast Asia? And the feed additives and antibiotics used in salmon farming? With oysters, it's different. No feed or medicine is involved. And they contribute more to habitat enhancement than they do to habitat degradation.

Oysters can benefit waterways by simply doing what they do: filter water (as much as fifty gallons per day for large oysters). Their first priority is sourcing nutrients, but in doing so they're also cleaning the water. Clear water allows more sunlight to reach other organisms, which can help them thrive. Plus, the oysters themselves and the beds they inhabit create habitats for other creatures. And their processing of water helps move nutrients they don't require farther down the water column to appreciative species below.

All that, and they're delicious too. It's little wonder that countless agencies and organizations now rally to offer support to oyster populations. Habitat restoration, more intent management of water quality controls, further ecological research, enhancement and expansion of shellfish beds, public outreach about ecosystem issues—these are among the efforts to ensure oysters and other shellfish remain a dynamic part of the local seascape. The Washington Shellfish Initiative, as an example, was established to "protect and enhance" shellfish resources in the state. As I completed research on this book, work was underway in California and Oregon to develop shellfish initiatives for those states as well.

Growing oysters starts, for the most part, in land-based hatcheries where oysters spawn to create larvae. (Some oysters raised on Pacific Coast farms do begin life from "wild set"—naturally occurring spawn—

The Life & Times of the Modern Oyster

but it's not the norm.) When the larvae are large enough to settle, they attach to a hard surface on which they will develop their shells. If it's a whole oyster shell (called a "cultch"), a number of oysters will grow in a cluster from that shell. These oysters will generally be shucked for meat to be jarred. But some growers will break up the clusters when near maturity and toss the individual oysters back out to the bed to grow solo for a spell.

If the grower wants individually formed oysters ideal for the prime half-shell market, they will provide the larvae with oyster shells that are ground instead of whole. Each grain of the ground shell is large enough for just one single larva—which at that point measures about 0.3 millimeters—to attach itself, the perfect single-occupant home.

Hatchery facilities are expensive to develop and maintain, so there aren't many of them. Many oyster growers on the Pacific Coast rely on purchased larvae or "seed oysters" (spat oysters ready to be planted on an oyster bed) that they'll raise on their own property. Given the meroir effect, oysters take on distinctions of their home bed even when coming from a common seed source.

There are two basic approaches for growing oysters—bottom culture and off-bottom culture, with numerous variations and hybrids among them. Some oyster vendors and menus will reference the growing method as one element of the oyster's character. Based on the growing method chosen and other variables that are at play, cultured oysters will be harvested at about two to four years of age.

Bottom culture can be as simple as scattering juvenile oysters across a tideflat, letting nature do the work, and then coming back in a few years to harvest mature oysters. The oysters that survive predators, storms, exposure, and other challenges will be sturdy and resilient. You'll often see these oysters referred to as "beach grown."

Bottom culture may also be done in broad, flat mesh bags attached to the ground; these oysters will still be bottom-raised but will have been secured and protected to some degree, making them a little less sturdy than beach grown. Some growers opt for the combination bag-to-beach method to gain the best of both approaches.

Among off-bottom options, longline is a common version. The cultch oysters with baby oysters attached are connected to ropes suspended a foot or two above the sea bottom in long rows. Or the oyster spat could go into mesh bags set on a rack raising them above the bottom. Other oysters grow suspended in lantern nets or trays from buoys or rafts, fully submerged 24/7. These methods provide oysters with more equal access to the plankton passing by, so they tend to grow more quickly than their bottom-culture counterparts. But they also tend to have less-sturdy shells when they don't get beach time.

With the advent of "tumbled" oysters, farmers can employ a technique that allows them to make up for limits traditional methods may have, while also customizing their product. Tumbling may be done by systems that amplify the tide's natural flow to more forcefully agitate the oysters within a bag or a bin. Floats attached to the outer edge of the bag will raise it upward with a high tide, then the bag will float downward when the tide recedes, so the oysters get tide tumbled twice each day. Other methods involve temporarily bringing the oysters on shore to tumble in a big cylindrical machine (think of your clothes dryer, without the hot air).

What tumbling accomplishes is breaking off just the fine outer edge of the oyster's shell. This elicits an instinct in the oyster to replenish that shell, which, over time, develops a more deeply cupped oyster with plumper meat. In modifying the architecture of the shell in that way, there is also invariably change in its design: these tumbled shells have less fluting and frilly layers, and instead have a smooth surface.

SEASONALITY

Oysters are produced year-round in most growing regions along the Pacific Coast. However, they are at their best, crispest, and most plump when conditions are cold, which is why we often associate the winter and early spring months with prime oyster time. That is when you are likely to see the most oysters in the greatest variety available in stores and on menus.

Warming water temperatures are generally what prompts spawning in oysters, the time when they commit energy to dispensing eggs and sperm, which is why oysters are often, at least traditionally, shunned during the summer months. There's nothing harmful about eating spawning oysters; they simply have thinner, softer meat that many find undesirable.

Contemporary oyster farming alleviates much of this concern with the option of raising oysters that are called "triploids," which have been bred to be essentially sterile so they don't respond to spawning impulses over the summer. And some varieties don't spawn on the same schedule as others, such as Kumamotos, making them great over the summer. Plus, colder waters, as those up in Alaska or in deeper parts of bays, prohibit spawning impulses completely.

PACIFIC

EASTERN

EUROPEAN FLAT

OLYMPIA

KUMAMOTO

Pacific (*Crassostrea gigas*)

Though not native to the West Coast of North America, the Pacific oyster has become by far the most significant species grown in the region, and it is grown around the world as well. As native Olympia oysters began disappearing in the early twentieth century, the Pacific oyster was brought from Japan to see if it might take well to these waters. It did, and it also grew larger and more quickly than Olympias, soon becoming the dominant local oyster. The exact size and shape of a Pacific oyster will vary depending on where and how it was grown, but it often has a distinctive fluted—sometimes almost ruffly—shell.

You will seldom see an oyster sold as simply a "Pacific oyster," particularly if there are any other oysters around. Given this prolific species' geographic spread, there would be a lot with the same name. Pacific oysters most often get to be known by the place name of where they were harvested, such as Dabob Bay or Pickering Passage oysters. Though nongeographic names work too, as with Chelsea Gem oysters from Washington's Eld Inlet or Summer Ice oysters from British Columbia's Jervis Inlet.

Kumamoto (*Crassostrea sikamea*)

The Kumamoto oyster is another transplant to the West Coast from Japan. The Kumamoto is small, rarely longer than two inches, with a deep cup and firm, mild meat that is easy to enjoy. Little wonder Kumamotos (or "Kumos" to aficionados) are so popular and make for a great starter oyster for those first slurps. These oysters hold up well over summer because they don't follow the same spawning schedule as most Pacific oysters. They also didn't naturalize to this region's waters as well as Pacifics did, requiring more protection and care, so only a handful of producers farm Kumamotos.

Regardless of where they are grown, these oysters will generally be sold simply as "Kumamoto oysters," though some oyster bar menus or retail displays may list at least the state, if not the bay, from which the Kumamoto was harvested.

Olympia (*Ostrea lurida*)

The Olympia oyster is small in size (under two inches long) and big in flavor (often coppery metallic like its *Ostrea* kin, the European flat oyster). The Olympia is the only oyster native to the West Coast of North America and was named Washington State's official oyster in 2014. Native populations were nearly wiped out completely by the mid-1900s, thanks to overharvest and a toxic environment propelled in part by flourishing pulp and paper mills. But extensive and continuing efforts to revive Olympia populations all along the Pacific Coast have shown success, so the oyster is showing up more again.

Fragile little things, Olympias take some TLC in their rearing and also grow slowly, despite their diminutive size, so all in all, growing Olympias is not the most compelling of business prospects. But the payoff can be big, as these little guys are cherished as one of the premier specialty oysters available. Fans are generally opportunistic, indulging whenever the oysters appear.

Eastern (*Crassostrea virginica*)

As the name suggests, the Eastern oyster is native to the East Coast of North America where it is a prolific species that, like the Pacific, is most often sold by distinctive place names. When it became clear the native Olympia oyster stocks were waning in the late nineteenth century, the Eastern was the first attempted replacement oyster. Shiploads of seed oysters were sent from the East Coast, and they did pretty well for some time and were well received. But transcontinental seed sourcing proved inefficient and costly, and before long the Pacific came along, with growers turning attention to that easily acclimated variety. For many years little or no Eastern oysters were grown on the West Coast.

The revival of Pacific-grown Eastern oysters came in the past couple of decades, with both Hog Island Oyster Co. on Tomales Bay in California and Taylor Shellfish Farms on Totten Inlet in Washington growing *C. virginica* oysters. In fact, the great-grandfather of Bill Taylor (vice president of Taylor Shellfish) was growing them on Totten Inlet over a century ago. The modern Totten Inlet Virginica has come to be one of the favorites among oyster bar devotees.

European flat (*Ostrea edulis*)

The European flat oyster is the pinnacle variety typically associated with the northwest of France, where the region's famous Belon oysters are considered a special delicacy. The species has been gravely challenged in recent years by a parasite. While this species produces delicious results grown on the Pacific Coast, it is slow growing and delicate and its seed is hard to come by, so some local growers who once grew European flats have cut back on production. Lopez Island Shellfish on

Lopez Island in Washington recently released, however, the Shoal Bay flat, using seed produced there on the farm. And down in California, Hog Island Oyster Co. has been working to propagate seed from their own brood stock. Their flat oyster goes by the name French Hog and is in limited production, though you may see it occasionally on their oyster bar menus. Like Belons, European flat oysters grown here have a pronounced and bold flavor, rich with coppery minerals, which is a cherished characteristic for enthusiasts.

PACIFIC COAST GROWING REGIONS

I'll start with my home state of Washington, which is the biggest producer of oysters on the Pacific Coast, not to mention one of the largest in the country. A glance at a map paired with a basic understanding of what oysters look for in a home (protected bodies of nutrient-rich saltwater with doses of fresh water for balance), and you'll see that the Puget Sound, Hood Canal, Willapa Bay, and other smaller waterways are lavish oyster territory.

California, a state with countless other agricultural resources, has a different geography with fewer oyster-friendly bays. Humboldt Bay is the top oyster-producing area in the state, which, along with Tomales Bay, represents the bulk of oyster production in California. There are also some oyster producers farther south, including in and around Morro Bay. San Francisco Bay was, in its time, a resource, but the supply of native oysters there quickly dwindled during the gold rush era, both from overharvest and because of ecological disruption from mining operations.

Efforts are underway to reestablish the bay's marine health, including reviving habitats for oysters.

Oregon's ocean coast is rather linear, though it does feature a handful of bays that are conducive to growing oysters. The most prolific among them are Tillamook Bay and Coos Bay, followed closely by Yaquina Bay. Netarts Bay also produces oysters, though it has limited production simply based on its resource capacity. Netarts Bay is, however, home to one of the largest oyster hatcheries on the Pacific Coast, Whiskey Creek Shellfish Hatchery.

British Columbia is a large province with quite a lot of coastline, but its oyster-growing production is concentrated primarily in and around the Strait of Georgia, particularly in the Comox Valley area. Over half of the province's oyster production comes from Baynes Sound. The second most productive area is to the north near Lund, from Okeover Inlet, Quadra Island, and Cortes Island growing areas nearby. There are even some hearty souls who work on the western, more rugged side of Vancouver Island.

And yes, there are oysters in Alaska, the great land of seafood. But while so many other species thrive that far north, it's not a natural habitat for oysters, since the waters are too cold to induce them to spawn naturally. Growers there begin with oyster seed (which may need to come from the Lower 48) and they must be a little patient, because the cold water temperatures slow growth. But the lush waters then go on to produce delicious oysters with bright and vivid flavor. And given the cold waters and lack of spawning, they're also an ideal year-round selection.

THE ACIDIFICATION FACTOR

One of the newest and most challenging realities facing oyster (and other shellfish) growers is ocean acidification. As a scientific study, change in the pH levels of ocean water isn't new. But it wasn't until the first decade of this century that increased attention was given to the connection between the pH change and the die-off of larval oysters.

Carbon emissions, as it happens, don't only float skyward toward the atmosphere but are also absorbed into the planet's waters. For a number of years that was considered to be a good thing, since it decreased the amount of CO_2 in the atmosphere. But increased CO_2 in the water raises the level of the water's acidity, which is a problem for shellfish and other calcium-dependent creatures. The chemical reactions associated with these changes impede the oyster's ability to form a viable shell, a process that begins within hours of hatching. Without that initial shell, the oyster's chances of survival dissolve.

For hatcheries (which may raise their own oysters as well as sell larvae or more mature seed to other growers), adapting to current conditions includes careful study and modification of their operations. In cooperation with scientists, they are making strides to assure continued production of healthy oysters by establishing conditions under which larvae are able to produce strong shells. Once an oyster's initial shell is well established, the oyster will mature and grow an increasingly larger shell in the natural environment with little issue.

Much has yet to be learned about ocean acidification and how we can mitigate its effects on the health of marine life. What's been seen so far has been eye-opening and has motivated a great deal of scientific investigation and experimentation that will be underway for some time.

"Don't throw out the brine, that's the best part!" This I overheard in an oyster bar as an oyster devotee instructed a friend who apparently was a slurping novice. It was said with kindness, certainly, but with an emphatic punctuation that left no doubt. Oyster lovers are a passionate bunch, and they invariably want to share that passion with others. So if you're not currently an oyster fiend, find someone who is and just go along for the ride!

Oyster consumption venues come in all forms. The simplest is the personal shuck-and-slurp, with your feet planted anywhere near a good source of oysters. No cooking to do, no manners to mind, no reservations to make. You, an oyster, and an oyster knife. The other end of the spectrum comes in white-tablecloth finery, oysters perched on an elegant porcelain plate, maybe a splash of champagne mignonette or a dab of caviar. In between? There are endless options for how and where you might eat oysters. One benefit of living in such prolific oyster-growing territory is that they show up in a wide range of dining experiences.

The ultimate oyster-centric destination is an oyster bar. Conviviality is a large part of the oyster bar experience. It's akin to the best of sushi-eating experiences, when you're sitting at the sushi bar and chatting with the sushi chef about what's newest/freshest/most interesting among that evening's selections. It's a completely different experience from sitting at a table twenty feet away and ordering off the menu.

The same is true in an oyster bar. You can chat with the shucker about what oysters from the roster are the plumpest and most delicious that day, ask about distinctions between the varieties, and pick up some shucking tips. And maybe, if you're in the right place at the right time, you might get a shucker's treat, like the Sumo Kumamoto (an older, slightly larger version of the beloved oyster bar choice) I was given at a Taylor Oyster Bar one afternoon when they'd just been delivered. A half dozen on the half shell can be delightful in any restaurant setting, but it's at the oyster bar where the eater is oyster-engaged at a higher level.

Now it's time to think about eating some of these briny delights. And I must lead off with a visit to Swan Oyster Depot in San Francisco. Frills? None here. Nor the most comfortable seats, nor much room for your food on the slender counter shared by you and a dozen-plus others. The wait's generally very long out on the sidewalk. It's cash only. So many things could count against this place. But once you sit down, the geniality, the simplicity of the menu (nothing cooked to order, most is raw or precooked and chilled), and the quality of the seafood draw you in. You go here in the right frame of mind and ready to slip into Swan time for a unique oyster (and crab, shrimp, cured salmon, etc.) experience. They've been doing something right for over a hundred years.

For the Pacific Coast oyster bar with the most long-standing and interesting history, though, my vote goes to Dan & Louis Oyster Bar in Portland. It may not have been in operation quite as long as Swan has, but its roots go back earlier. Oregon Oyster Farms on Yaquina Bay dates to 1910 (a few years earlier under a different name) and owner Louis Charles Wachsmuth based his business operations in downtown Portland. By the late 1910s he'd opened a small side business of selling shucked oysters—low overhead, minimal staff needed. Over the next couple of decades the offerings grew to include oyster stew, seafood cocktails, and seafood salads. It grew too into a dedicated space nearby, operating as the full-service Dan & Louis Oyster Bar by the late 1930s.

Dan & Louis Oyster Bar is still in operation today, and it maintains a strong dose of authentic nostalgia. The oysters are still great—fresh and served simply as they should be. Other parts of the menu may be less inspiring, but the place remains true to its heritage, for which—in my mind—they deserve great credit. If they or Swan Oyster Depot decided to revamp their spaces for some modern panache, the character and local culture they represent would be, in my opinion, lost. I very much hope both are around for decades to come. Anyone can open a new oyster bar. But no one can open one that's got a century or so under its belt. I'm a big proponent of appreciating and supporting both the old and the new.

One thing that baffles me about Seattle is that it has no Swan Oyster Depot, no Dan & Louis Oyster Bar. It's a city with plenty of seashore, a long commercial seafood history, and many generations of devoted seafood lovers—and yet our oyster bar heritage is limited. It took three-quarters into the twentieth century to see oysters register much on Seattle's culinary radar. A *Seattle Times* article from December 1978 written by John Hinterberger discusses the then proliferation of oyster-slurping venues, including F.X. McRory's, Shuckers Oyster Bar, and the soon-to-be-opened Emmett Watson's Oyster Bar, all of which are still in operation today. But in that context he points out the interesting fact that "a mere three years ago . . . Seattle had no oyster bar."

But new oyster bars? Seattle has those in spades. The first-generation wave includes the aforementioned trio, with Elliott's Oyster House and The Brooklyn joining in the 1980s. The latest spate is quite a dynamic bunch with The Walrus and the Carpenter, three locations of Taylor Oyster Bars, Bitter/Raw, Ballard Annex Oyster House, Little Gull at Westward, and the bar at Blueacre, among others. All along the Pacific coast, you'll find many dozens of places like these—from L & E Oyster Bar in Los Angeles

to Rodney's Oyster House in Vancouver—where longtime devotees and newbies alike can get their fill of just-shucked treasures. And you'll find Pacific Coast oysters showing up around the country too, from the venerable Grand Central Oyster Bar in New York City to smaller neighborhood spots. Oyster fans have plenty of opportunity to slurp eastern and western varieties together to appreciate their distinct characteristics.

Even the newest kids on the block can manage to feel rather like old souls. There's not much to improve about the classic art of choosing outstanding oysters, shucking them with care, perching them on ice, and giving them to appreciative customers. At least not if you're doing it right.

Oyster accoutrements range from lemon wedges and cocktail sauce to freshly grated horseradish and mignonette. Maybe on occasion it's a zesty frozen topping. Or signature variations on the mignonette theme. At Blueacre in Seattle, I've had a soy-ginger sauce and a house cocktail sauce made with fresh horseradish. At Hog Island oyster bars in California, they serve their signature Hog Wash sauce made with rice vinegar, shallot, jalapeño, cilantro, and lime juice.

And you're certainly not limited to raw slurping. One of the most enjoyable things about this growing array of oyster outlets is seeing what else is on tap—how they round out their raw bar menu. Because after that first dozen or two oysters, you may be ready for something else. Like other raw seafood, ceviche, smoked fish, fried or baked oysters, seafood cocktails, chowder, maybe some pickled vegetables, and interesting salads. You can compose a pretty phenomenal meal from among the offerings. An oyster bar is the perfect destination to enjoy some great food, check out new oysters you haven't tried before, gain some ideas for things you might want to cook at home, and generally feed your oyster inspirations.

IN THE KITCHEN

BUYING & STORING OYSTERS

The key consideration when shopping for oysters is to buy them from a merchant that goes through a decent amount of oysters. Frequent turnover means a higher likelihood of getting a fresher product—not to mention that it means they're familiar with handling and selling oysters. If the pile of in-shell oysters looks a little forlorn and haphazard to one side of a seafood case, rather than piled on ice and arranged with care, it might be a clue they're not prime oyster sellers.

Direct yourself to specialty seafood markets, markets that have tanks or dedicated shellfish displays (Asian markets in particular often have great seafood selections), and supermarkets that clearly go out of their way to bring in top-quality product and take good care of it until it's in your hands. Some farmers' markets may have oyster farmers among their vendors, a wonderful direct-from-the-producer option. And if you don't have these options where you live, know that oysters are surprisingly resilient travelers, and you can order them to be shipped a day or two from harvest to your doorstep (see Oyster Shopping Guide, page 135).

When shopping for jarred oysters, check the "sell by" date on the jar, which is generally a couple of weeks from the date it was packed. Regardless of that date, once you open the container you should use the oysters within a day or so. Also check that the packaging is securely sealed and there's no leaking or punctures (as may be the case with a plastic tub). The oysters should be plump and evenly colored, and fully submerged in liquor, which should be clear.

For in-shell oysters, these are alive and need to stay alive until you prepare them. Some stores may have them in saltwater tanks. But out of water, oysters hold up quite well in the right conditions: cold (35 to 38 degrees F), with air to breathe, and a moist environment.

Live oysters in the shell don't come with a sell-by date stamped on them, but each bag of oysters is required by law in both the United States and Canada to have a shellfish tag attached. It includes information such as identification of the producer, description of the product, date of harvest, and place of harvest. Whatever business entity receives the oysters must keep the tag available for viewing upon request as long as that batch of product lasts, then keep the tag on file for ninety days from receipt. Don't be afraid to ask to see that tag!

To ensure in-shell oysters are alive, the shells should be tightly closed; like clams and mussels, they may gape a bit on occasion but they don't gape quite as much. The shells should definitely close when tapped, and if not, toss them out. A bit of chipping on the outer edge of the oyster shell is of little concern, but if any chips or cracks expose the oyster interior, discard that one as well.

If there's a hollow sound that results from tapping an oyster with another oyster or some other small hard item, it's likely the oyster has lost much of its liquor. Pass on these if you have a chance before purchase. Follow your senses and your gut instinct. If you open an oyster and it looks small in the shell, deflated, and not plump and moist, it's not in prime form. It may not be bad to eat, but it won't be a great eating experience. And if you open an oyster that smells off or funky, don't hesitate to toss it out.

When you get your shelled oysters home, refrigerate them right away. (If it's a warm day and/or you'll not be returning directly home from the store, ask for a bag or two of crushed ice at the seafood counter to keep the oysters cold in transit.) The paper or plastic wrapping should be opened up, allowing the oysters to breathe. The oysters will be best enjoyed soon after purchase, but live oysters in their shells, stored properly, will hold well for three or four days (or longer, but don't push it).

You've got a few options for storing oysters in your refrigerator, depending on space available and how many oysters you have. The easiest, I find, is to put the oysters in a colander, set the colander inside a bowl just large enough to hold it, and cover the oysters with a damp (but not dripping wet) kitchen towel. Try to arrange the oysters in a vaguely horizontal (cupped-side down) fashion to preserve the maximum amount of liquor. Or, if you've got the refrigerator space for it, you could lay the oysters out flat in a rimmed baking sheet or large oblong baking dish, covered with a damp towel. Lastly, if you have a lot of oysters and/or you can spare the space, empty out one of the bin drawers from the refrigerator, put some crumpled newspaper in the bottom (to help soak up liquid that invariably will collect), arrange the oysters in it (usually still in their bags, but be sure the bags are open to allow them to breathe), and top with that damp towel.

Some folks swear by storing their oysters with ice, which is fine—but not really necessary in the refrigerator. It's important, if doing so, that the oysters are arranged in a way to ensure they will not be sitting in the water that runs off the melting ice. Oysters do not survive long in fresh water.

Any time you are cooking or serving the oysters in their shells, rinse them well first. If they're particularly dirty, scrub them with a stiff brush under cool running water. But if just moderately dirty, you can put them in a colander under cold running water and rather aggressively shake and toss the oysters so they knock against each other to help dislodge dirt and other debris. Don't submerge the oysters in water.

To store jarred oysters, be sure they stay fully chilled in the refrigerator until needed, sitting upright to avoid leaking.

SIZING THEM UP

One of the more interesting, and frankly frustrating, things I realized in working on this book is that there aren't a lot of industry standards with regard to sizes assigned to oysters for consumer sales.

When it comes to jarred oysters, container sizes vary among producers, but eight-, ten-, and sixteen-ounce jars are quite common. Though some brands may have other offerings, the sizes of oysters in those jars will generally range from yearling, on the smaller end, to extra-small, small, and medium. I haven't seen jarred oysters larger than medium and, given how big some of those mediums are, I think it's just as well.

It would be delightful if we knew, for example, that every ten-ounce jar of small oysters was going to contain eight oysters, but that's not the case. Some jars may have seven, others nine. And those oysters may not be of exactly the same size. In many recipes, one oyster more or less, or incon-sistent sizing, isn't necessarily a deal breaker, but distribution among your dinner guests may just not be as even as hoped.

Oysters sold in the shell may not have any size listed, though a glance will give you an idea of their relative size. Generally they run from yearling/petite to extra-small, small, medium, and large. The latter are sometimes called barbecue or grill oysters, since they're beyond most oyster eater's capacity to eat any other way. I think of them as knife-and-fork oysters. We'll seldom see the jumbo oysters, larger still, which are prized in Asia and tend to go directly to that devoted market.

Which to choose, in the shell or in the jar? Jarred oysters are certainly convenient to use in any recipe for which you won't be cooking or serving the oysters in the shell. However, you can save shells after one meal, clean them very well, and later add jarred oysters to them for baking or grilling in the shell. For slurping on the half shell, live in-shell oysters are the only way to go.

For many recipes, either form will work, so the ingredient lists may offer options for both freshly shucked (you buy the oysters in the shell and shuck them yourself) or jarred (my general term for any container of preshucked oysters). Again, jarred will be quicker. But when you want to be more certain of the number and size of oyster you'll have to work with, in the shell gives you more control. It does mean shucking (see Shucking Oysters, page 31), but the benefit will be twofold: greater assurance of the oysters being the same size and you can buy exactly the number of oysters you need.

I haven't found much similarity between the sizes assigned to oys-ters in the shell and those in a jar. Generally the jarred version is larger:

a "medium" from the jar is bigger than the meat just shucked from a "medium" oyster. This is why I may call for small to medium in-shell oysters or extra-small to small jarred oysters in the recipes.

SHUCKING OYSTERS

The art of opening oysters has many approaches. Half-shell pros often shuck simply holding the oyster and knife in their hands, not working on a counter. To me, it feels really awkward to shuck without a solid surface on which to securely hold the oyster. But likewise, one pro friend tried to show others the counter technique, and it just didn't feel right to him. So to each his own; either method works and will become comfortable once you get the hang of it. Just take some precautions as you go.

Protecting your hands is of number-one importance. Gloves are made just for this purpose, composed of rubbery material or steel mesh. For in-hand shuckers, a glove is a must! It's not only to protect from potential knife-to-hand contact, but also because many oyster shells have quite sharp edges that can cut just by holding them firmly in your hand. Items already in your kitchen can be used too, such as a heavy kitchen towel or oven mitt.

Next up is the oyster knife. I prefer using one that has a blade more slender and long than broad and stubby; I find it easier to maneuver in and around the oyster. Be sure the handle has some texture to it to help ensure a good grip even when your hand is wet. Never use a paring knife or other sharp kitchen knife for shucking oysters, as the thin blades may not be strong enough and you risk greater injury should the blade slip in the wrong direction. That being said, an oyster knife should have a fine enough

Having initially slipped the oyster knife into the hinged joint at the back of the oyster, carefully slide the blade across the top shell to separate it from the top side of the adductor muscle.

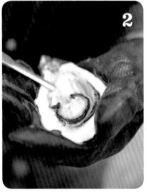

With the top shell now removed, slide the blade under the oyster to sever the bottom side of the adductor muscle.

edge to cut, rather than mangle, the adductor muscle from the shell.

Once you've got your hand protection, a good knife, and some outstanding oysters in your possession, it's time to shuck.

I opt for the counter method and use a thick, terry-cloth kitchen towel to hold the oyster securely. Fold the towel lengthwise in thirds or quarters to produce a few layers of thickness. Set the oyster on the towel near one end, with its cupped-side down and pointed hinge end facing your dominant hand. Fold the rest of the towel up and over the oyster, holding the oyster down toward the rounded end with your non-dominant hand and leaving the hinge still exposed.

Firmly grasp the oyster knife and use the tip of the knife to wedge carefully between the oyster halves at the hinge. Sometimes this is easy, and sometimes it takes more determination. But keep at it and you will find the hinge gives and the knife tip will slip between the shells. The trick here—and I still fail at this now and then—is to have just the tip of the knife slip in, rather than barging in with the whole blade. The latter is not a catastrophe, but it often means the oyster meat will be a bit marred as a result. It's still perfectly edible, though.

Once the blade tip has slipped in, turn the knife handle to pry apart the shells a bit more. Then run the blade of the knife flat against the top shell of the oyster, separating the adductor muscle. The muscle is in the top-right quarter portion of the oyster relative to the hinge, to give you an idea of where to direct your efforts. Lift off and discard the top shell and gently slide the knife blade under the oyster as well to slice through the lower adductor muscle and fully separate the oyster. If you're serving it on the half shell and nicked the oyster earlier, you can flip the oyster over in its shell so the other side is facing (I won't tell).

VARIATIONS ON THE SHUCKING THEME

There are myriad ways to shuck an oyster. Julia Child, for one, was a proponent of the bottle opener, also known as a church key. This is the simple old-school metal tool with one flatter end for flipping off bottle caps and a pointy end for puncturing cans. The idea is to insert that pointy end into the hinge spot and apply pressure to pop open the shell. I have found this works well on oysters that have just-right hinge access but is less effective on oddly shaped or harder-to-open shells. And you'll still need a small knife for cutting the adductor muscle.

Far from old-school is the liquid nitrogen approach, or cryo-shucking. Nathan Myhrvold and his culinary team (creators of the massive six-volume *Modernist Cuisine* released in 2011, a project I was lucky enough to be part of) developed a technique by which a very quick and very cold freeze forces the adductor muscle to seize with virtually no impact to the rest of the oyster meat. About fifteen seconds in liquid nitrogen (roughly negative 325 degrees F) is all it takes. The oyster is left to return to a "normal" chilled temperature in the refrigerator, in which time the adductor muscle releases from the shell and the oyster is essentially self-shucked.

Then there are what I can only consider to be overengineered contraptions, oyster shucking tools that are inflexible (not all oysters are the same—sizes, hinges, shell types vary) and too unitasker for my interest. And they tend to be expensive. For your money, get a good oyster knife, learn to shuck, and spend the rest on delicious oysters instead.

Oysters are high in zinc, which tends to immediately bring to mind the oysters' longstanding reputation as an elixir of love. But most nutritionists tend to focus more on the fact that zinc helps promote a healthy immune system, maintain our sense of smell and taste, and build proteins, among other benefits. In fact, oysters contain more zinc than any other food.

Other nutritional plusses include being a very good source of protein, iron, vitamin B12, and omega-3 fatty acids, while relatively low in overall fat, calories, and sodium (yes, sodium, despite thinking of them as salty-briny). And though oysters contain what may seem like a high level of cholesterol (about forty-two milligrams per three-ounce serving), there are newer understandings of how the cholesterol we consume (what's known as dietary cholesterol) impacts—or may not, as recent findings have shown—the cholesterol in our bodies (blood cholesterol). This helps temper the oyster's oft-cited reputation as being bad for cholesterol-sensitive diets. Their nutrient profile has been found in at least one study to support the "good" HDL cholesterol levels in our bodies and can help lower the "bad" LDL cholesterol.

One of the dietary concerns related to oysters in this part of the world is *Vibrio parahaemolyticus*, a naturally occurring bacterium that—in large concentration—can cause gastrointestinal illness. It proliferates in warmer waters, which in these parts tend to occur in shallower bays and estuaries, primarily in the hottest months of summer. Waters on the West Coast of the United States don't produce *Vibrio vulnificus*, a more virulent form found in the East. Thorough cooking (reaching an internal temperature of 145 degrees F for a duration of fifteen seconds, measured using an instant-read thermometer) eliminates the harmful effects of *V. parahaemolyticus.*

Under the auspices of the National Shellfish Sanitation Program, a number of federal and state agencies in the United States participate in close monitoring of oyster habitats as well as supporting other mechanisms—such as the shellfish tag every commercial bag of oysters must include—to do all they can to ensure a safe oyster eating experience. When a problem is detected, oyster harvest in the area is closed until water temperatures drop to safe levels.

Be sure to only buy oysters from a reputable merchant that's selling them from licensed growers. Recreational harvest of shellfish is managed by state and provincial departments of fish and wildlife (or game, as the case may be). Be sure to check these agencies for information about harvest allowances, license requirements, seasonal openings, etc. before harvesting any oysters yourself.

Consuming raw or undercooked shellfish can carry risks for women who are pregnant, the very young, the very old, and those with compromised immune systems.

WHAT TO DRINK WITH OYSTERS

I'll start by saying that I'm not a big proponent of following "rules" regarding what beverage goes with what food. We all have vastly different palates and preferences; we taste foods and flavor combinations in distinctly personal ways. So I believe that "whatever you want" is a perfectly valid answer to the perennial "what should I drink with [fill in the blank]?" question.

That being said, there are some guidelines that come from objective consideration of the ingredients at hand and what's been learned from past experience. For the sake of this exercise, I'll consider the ingredient to be a raw oyster on the half shell. As with any food, the "what to drink" question is answered as much by how it's prepared and what other ingredients are added as by the main ingredient you start with. A creamy oyster stew (page 112), grilled oysters with tomato and bacon (page 86), and pan-fried oysters on a salad (page 99) take us down different paths based on their preparations. That exploration gets at universal principles of beverage pairing that are beyond the scope of this book. I realize many oyster slurpers do like to add a squeeze of lemon or tiny drizzle of mignonette, which in small doses shouldn't impact these pairing ideas that follow. Those oyster accents are accomplishing the same thing that well-paired beverages will do: they add a touch of savory acidity and bracing character to complement the rich, briny flavor of the oyster.

So let's consider what a beautiful, just-shucked half-shell oyster brings to the table. In broad terms, its flavor elements might include varying degrees of minerality, richness, brininess, vegetal flavors (cucumber, seaweed, lettuce, herbs), hints of green melon, and some earthy notes.

Complementary flavors to look for in potential beverage partners would include tart, crisp, mineral, citrus, herbal, spicy, vegetal, and smoky characteristics. As with any good partnership, ideally the two components will elevate each other when combined, with neither—no matter how delicious it may be—dominating the other. Though, granted, where "dynamic and bold partnership" ends and "one-sided domination" begins is a matter of opinion.

Half-shell oysters are about as simple as it gets, and they often lead us toward serving equally simple sips alongside: a glass of bubbly or white wine, icy vodka, chilled beer. There's little risk of competitive flavors, especially when leaning toward selections that are dry and brisk, not fruity, sweet, or overpowering.

Even though two of my oyster-loving friends, cocktail experts Robert Hess and Audrey Saunders, have an incredibly well-stocked bar and the talent to whip up a cocktail to suit any occasion, Robert says, "We will typically drink Champagne with oysters. The acid and texture of the bubbles provide a perfect counterpoint, and the crisp yet subtle flavor of the Champagne doesn't compete with the brininess of the oysters. It's all about finding the right balance."

There is a lot to be said for Champagne and dry sparkling wines as perhaps the ultimate pairing for oysters—including most of the recipes in this book.

Another friend, oyster evangelist Jon Rowley, has made a fine art out of finding the best still wines to pair with oysters. Over twenty years ago he established the Pacific Coast Oyster Wine Competition, inspired by a passage from Ernest Hemingway's *A Moveable Feast*, part of which reads: "I ate the oysters with their strong taste of the sea and their faint metallic taste that the cold white wine washed away, leaving only the taste of the sea . . ." Jon reads the full passage at the start of each judging session as something of an anthem to put the judges in the right frame of mind.

Like my cohort judges, I chew an oyster with each sample, sip a bit of the wine, and see how well they play together on my palate, looking for a wine that "finishes clean and that exalts the oyster by not getting in the way of the next oyster," as Jon directs. From past judging notes, my favorite wines included descriptions like "bright and mineral," "touch

of acid," "clean finish so oyster shines," and "refreshing and crisp." The wines that clashed most for me had strong floral and fruit characters. No points for any wine that bulldozed across the tongue and wiped out the oyster flavor.

This competition has featured wines from Washington, Oregon, and California—in celebration of the "what grows together, goes together" ethos. Among the wines that make the top-ten list, sauvignon blancs have been common, which echo one of the classic French oyster-wine choices, Sancerre—also made with sauvignon blanc grapes. Pinot gris/grigio (same grape, different name) wines are frequent winners as well, with an occasional dry chenin blanc.

It's hard to go wrong with a crisp, dry, slightly acidic white wine. Or a glass of Champagne. But you want more variety than that, right? How about beer? As much as I love beer, it's not often the drink I pair with oysters. Maybe it is because my favorite beers are strong with hops, and I find their distinct floral-resin-bitter flavor overwhelms raw oysters. Lighter, brighter options like lagers and pilsners are great candidates. And, as unlikely as it may seem, sipping a stout alongside oysters has a huge following, particularly Guinness, which I imagine to be an especially enchanting pairing when slurping an Irish oyster on its home turf. (I'm putting that experience on my bucket list.) Some adventurous brewers going back decades have even produced stout made *with* oysters, as has the brewery at Spinnakers Gastro Brewpub in Victoria, British Columbia, using Hollie Wood oysters from Baynes Sound a bit up-island.

When it comes to spirits, I'm tempted to skip right over vodka and head straight to gin, because it has so much more flavor to contribute. Sampling vodka with half-shell oysters during my research, as part of a larger study of how different spirits fared in the oyster-pairing department, I thought it was fine. Clean and brisk, not unpleasant, no particular complaints. It just didn't contribute much.

Gin's prominent ingredient is juniper, and with its bracing, slightly evergreen character it is a good start for complementing oysters. From there, gins can contain any number of botanical ingredients that generally lean toward oyster compatibility. Not only do those botanicals mesh well with the oysters' natural flavor, the touch of brine from the oysters elevates the botanical character, like you'd expect from a pinch of salt in a recipe. I would only caution that gins with strong floral components might clash with, rather than complement, a raw oyster.

Another spirit that leaped quickly to mind was aquavit. Not dissimilar to gin, aquavit is a spirit flavored with spices and herbs. Also like gin, it can be made with a broad range of flavor combinations; I would lean toward those that include herbal and savory-spice elements (fennel, dill, coriander) rather than warm spices (allspice, star anise).

The spirit-pairing study I mentioned was casual in format but serious in intent. I invited Jake Kosseff, partner/wine director at Miller's Guild in Seattle, to join me and we settled in for an afternoon of experimenting. A couple dozen oysters at a time, with three or four spirits at a time, straight up, pure and simple. In addition to the vodka and gin noted, the other white spirit we tried was a blanco tequila, which we liked at least as much as the gin. Its slight earthiness tempered the brine a touch, and other flavors in the oysters became more pronounced. Both the oysters and the tequila tasted better together.

The big surprise as we moved through different spirits was how well brown spirits partnered with the raw oysters. I would have categorically dismissed the whole lot of them, from bourbon to single malt Scotch, believing them inherently overwhelming to that little nugget of briny delight. Not so fast.

The three Scotches we tried—one Lowland (Auchentoshan), one Speyside (Glenlivet), and one Islay (Laphroaig)—all fared astonishingly well. (Okay, I will admit the Laphroaig put me over the edge—under any circumstance it's just too powerful for me.) The Scotches' sharpness contrasts the richness of the oysters but with restraint. The lightly smoky-wood character from barrel aging lingers on the palate and melds nicely with lingering oyster flavors. And the peat factor brings a hint of saltiness to the Scotch that amplifies compatibility with the oyster's brine.

Cocktails are a whole other kettle of fish, and there are just too many options to distill here. But if you start with some of these spirits and consider the general array of flavors that complement oysters—citrus, spicy, herbal, tart, crisp—you get an idea of where to start with cocktail combinations.

RECIPES

RAW

OYSTER SHOTS—OR SHOOTERS, if you prefer—represent a broad category of serving options that need just a shucked oyster, a shot glass or something like it, and a splash of vividly flavored sauce. Given the name and the glass it's traditionally served in, no wonder many oyster shots include a dose of some alcohol as well. This booze-free version is appropriate for all age groups, though grown-ups can certainly spike theirs with a bit of vodka.

This is an occasion when evenly sized, freshly shucked small oysters are best. Drizzle a bit of their captured liquor into the tomato-juice mixture if you like.

ZIPPY OYSTER SHOTS

+ Chill 12 shot glasses or other small glasses in the refrigerator for about 1 hour before serving.

+ In a medium bowl, stir together the lemon juice and wasabi powder until evenly blended. Add the tomato juice, celery stalks, celery leaves, and a pinch of salt. Stir to evenly blend and let the juice mixture sit for about 15 minutes. Taste for seasoning, adding more salt if needed. If you want a stronger kick, blend another ½ teaspoon of the wasabi powder with 1 teaspoon of water and add it to the juice mixture. Let it sit again for 5 to 10 minutes.

+ Spoon a bit of the mixture into the bottom of each shot glass, which will help prevent the oyster from sticking to the glass. Add an oyster to each and top with the rest of the juice mixture. Serve right away.

MAKES 12 OYSTER SHOTS

2 tablespoons freshly squeezed lemon juice

1½ teaspoons wasabi powder, plus more to taste

1¼ cups tomato juice

¼ cup minced celery stalks

2 tablespoons minced celery leaves

Kosher salt

12 freshly shucked extra-small to small oysters (see Shucking Oysters, page 31), with their liquor

HOW TO SERVE
HALF-SHELL OYSTERS

The most ardent oyster fans I know recoil at the idea of splashing anything at all on the just-shucked gem sitting in its pearly shell. The only garnish they condone is the natural liquor in the shell with the oyster, which I can appreciate. I used to rarely, if ever, dip into the sauces offered on oyster platters. As is, you taste the very purest expression of oysterness that's available to us.

But as an open-minded oyster eater, I've come to work more variety into my slurping experiences and have realized that very light touches of complementary flavors can subtly brighten and accentuate the oyster's own flavor. A judicious dose is key. If you douse your oyster in mignonette or cocktail sauce and the flavor overwhelms the oyster, it's kind of missing the point.

The famous Portland-born gastronome James Beard had this to say about half-shell oysters in his *American Cookery* cookbook published in 1972: "At their best, oysters are eaten on the half shell with nothing to enhance them except lemon, a bit of grated fresh horseradish, or a mignonette pepper sauce. If you do not like the natural flavor of oysters, and find that you must cover them with quantities of red cocktail sauce, then perhaps you shouldn't be eating them."

Well, there you have it. I will take a different stance, though. For those new to raw slurping, for whom the first swallow of oyster just feels too big a leap, I say, sure, douse away during the getting-acquainted phase. Over time you can slowly decrease the douse to a tiny drizzle, increasing the prominence of the oyster itself.

What follows is a game plan for serving oysters on the half shell, with recipes for mignonettes, granités, and relishes as accompaniments (see pages 53 to 65). Note that for all the recipes, the yield is an approximation. The amount of topping used per oyster will vary with the slurper (from a drizzle to a douse) and with the size of the oysters. I recommend not pre-garnishing the oysters, instead setting the topping in a bowl alongside or in the center of the oyster tray, with a small spoon guests can use to accentuate their own just before slurping. An exception is the frozen granités, which you should distribute on the oysters and serve right away.

~~~~~~~~~~

Choose a rimmed tray on which you can set the just-shucked oysters. Something sturdy, watertight to contain ice melt, and with deep enough sides to hold at least an inch of ice. It can be a fancy tray if you have one, or a serving platter, but frankly once the ice and oysters are piled on, guests won't see much of the tray itself. And with delicious oysters to distract them, they won't much care what's holding them. I've used basic rimmed baking sheets at times. If you like the idea of those stainless-steel trays set on a raised stand like you see in oyster bars, check out a restaurant supply store in your area.

Ice is important for half-shell oysters that will be sitting for any time before guests enjoy them. For the oysters to nestle well into the ice— both to sit securely (not tipping out their luscious liquor) and to assure maximum shell contact with ice—it's best to use crushed ice rather than larger cubes. Ask at the seafood counter if they're willing to share some of their crushed ice with you.

Prepare the tray or platter with ice before you begin shucking, so the oysters can go directly onto the ice. The oysters can be shucked thirty to sixty minutes in advance and tucked into the refrigerator until ready to serve. This is a nice option so you can avoid shucking while your guests wait, particularly if you're not a whiz at it yet and would benefit from the lack of distraction to concentrate.

When it comes to the slurping itself, many prefer the timeless approach of lifting the oyster to bring the edge of its shell to their lips, then tipping the oyster and its liquor into their mouth. It's certainly the most sensory option: you feel the craggy shell in your hand and smell the distinct whiff of the fresh sea that's held in the shell before tasting the cold, plump oyster. Others prefer a daintier method of using a cocktail fork to lift the oyster from its shell, with the option of then sipping the liquor from the shell separately. Depending on how well you know your oyster-eating crowd, you may want to have some seafood forks on hand in case they prefer this latter option.

TYPES OF TOPPINGS

Mignonettes

This class of oyster sauce is known for brisk, bracing flavor, which serves as an ideal contrast to the rich and briny flavor of a raw oyster. Though mignonettes are most commonly made with vinegar, I offer one version with another oyster-friendly acidic ingredient: lemon juice (see page 55). They are very quick to make, and offer room for variation, whether using different vinegars (red, white, herb, sherry; I'd avoid sweeter balsamic) or different seasonings (pink peppercorns, fresh herbs, a bit of minced chile pepper).

Granités

Granités, sometimes called granitas, are a brisk and vibrant icy complement to half-shell oysters. Note that freezing temperatures dull the flavor of the ingredients, so the base mixture should be on the perky, flavorful side to begin with.

For freezing the mixtures, a shallow pan is ideal, so the mixture will freeze more quickly. I tend to use a pie pan, but it could be any number of vessels that are a couple inches deep and eight to ten inches across. Different materials can require different freezing times, so be mindful that exact times needed between stirs may vary. Generally, a metal pan quickens the freezing time relative to a glass pan or plastic container.

This is an easy technique but requires a bit of attention. You need to stir the mixture at regular intervals so it freezes with a flaky texture rather than freezing solid into a block. At first the icy flakes will be rather big, but as you stir over time and it freezes more, the texture will become more like coarse snow and lighten both in texture and color. If the granité does freeze solid, don't fret. Let it sit at room temperature long enough to soften again and continue with the freezing/stirring. Or you can break it into a smaller pieces and pulse in the food processor to finely chop; this will be best used right away.

Relishes

These oyster toppings are more substantial than the others in this chapter, with flavors that are vivid but not quite as pronounced as traditional mignonettes. Based on finely chopped vegetables, they also provide a bit of complementary crunch to play off the oyster. The uncooked relishes are vaguely reminiscent of salsa, and when you consider how diverse salsa variations are today—using ingredients from roasted tomatoes to pomegranate seeds—you get an idea of how diverse relish options can be for topping your oysters.

THE VERY CLASSIC mignonette commonly served with oysters is little more than red wine vinegar with minced shallot, the bright and brisk flavor a complement to the briny-rich oyster. You can make that by stirring together one-third cup red wine vinegar, two tablespoons minced shallot, and a grinding or two of black pepper. This twist on that classic first roasts the shallot whole to soften its sharp flavor, and uses white wine vinegar rather than red. Still brisk in flavor, it's a bit smoother than the original.

CHAMPAGNE VINEGAR-ROASTED SHALLOT MIGNONETTE

+ Preheat the oven to 400 degrees F.

+ Trim the root end from the shallot and peel away the papery outer skin. Wrap the shallot in a piece of aluminum foil and roast until it is tender when squeezed, about 30 minutes. Set aside to cool.

+ Finely chop 2 tablespoons of the cooled shallot. Save the rest for another use (vinaigrette dressing, rice, pasta).

+ In a small ramekin or other small serving dish, stir together the shallot, vinegar, and pepper to taste. The mignonette can be served right away, or allowed to sit for 1 to 2 hours. Refrigerate if making more than 2 hours in advance. (See the tips for serving raw oysters, page 48.)

MAKES ABOUT ½ CUP, *enough for about 4 dozen half-shell oysters*

1 medium shallot

⅓ cup champagne or white wine vinegar

Freshly ground black pepper

ROSEMARY AND OYSTERS may not seem the most natural of combinations. Rosemary is an herb with some punch, no doubt, but balanced with the bright lemon it makes a really delicious accent to oysters.

LEMON-ROSEMARY MIGNONETTE

✦ Put the rosemary in a small heatproof bowl, and pour the boiling water over. Set aside to steep for about 30 minutes. Drain, reserving both the rosemary and the water.

✦ In a small ramekin or other small serving dish, combine the lemon juice with 2 tablespoons of the rosemary water. Finely mince enough of the rosemary leaves to measure ¼ teaspoon and stir them into the lemon juice mixture. The flavors will be best if allowed to sit for 1 hour before serving. Refrigerate if making more than 2 hours in advance. (See the tips for serving raw oysters, page 48.)

MAKES ABOUT ½ CUP, *enough for about 4 dozen half-shell oysters*

1 tablespoon loosely packed fresh rosemary leaves

¼ cup boiling water

⅓ cup freshly squeezed lemon juice

BOTH FRESH AND PICKLED ginger add distinct flavor to this mignonette. Look for the thinly sliced ginger (often pink, sometimes a natural buff color) commonly served with sushi. It may be sold with other Asian ingredients in a refrigerated case, or you may find small condiment-size containers near prepared sushi.

RICE VINEGAR-GINGER MIGNONETTE

MAKES ABOUT ½ CUP, *enough for about 4 dozen half-shell oysters*

1 (2- to 3-inch) piece peeled fresh ginger (about 2 ounces), plus a bit more if needed

⅓ cup unseasoned rice vinegar

2 teaspoons finely minced pickled ginger

+ Finely grate the fresh ginger, using a Microplane grater if you have one. Put the grated ginger in a small fine sieve set over a small bowl and press on the ginger with the back of a spoon to extract the juice. You need about 2 teaspoons for this recipe; if you have a bit less and have no more ginger to juice, you can add a bit more of the pickled ginger instead.

+ In a small ramekin or other small serving dish, combine the ginger juice, rice vinegar, and pickled ginger. Refrigerate if making more than 2 hours in advance. (See the tips for serving raw oysters, page 48.)

ASIDE FROM CITRUS FRUITS, I am rarely inspired to combine oysters with fruit. This is a delicious exception, with the pear's mellow form of sweetness complemented by the punch of black pepper.

PEAR-BLACK PEPPER GRANITÉ

+ Coarsely chop the pear and puree it in a food processor with the water, vinegar, and pepper until very smooth. The mixture should have a pourable consistency; add a bit more water if needed.

+ Freeze and stir the mixture (see note below).

+ To serve, take the granité from the freezer and scrape it again with a fork to loosen it. Top each oyster with some of the granité and serve right away (see the tips for serving raw oysters, page 48).

MAKES ABOUT 3 CUPS, *enough for about 4 dozen half-shell oysters*

1 ripe pear, cored, seeded, and peeled (about 10 to 12 ounces)

½ cup water

3 tablespoons white wine vinegar

½ teaspoon freshly ground black pepper

BASIC FREEZING TECHNIQUE

Pour the granité mixture into a shallow pan, such as a 9-inch-diameter cake or pie pan. Clear a spot in your freezer where the pan can sit evenly, and freeze the mixture until it begins to set around the edges, 15 to 25 minutes. Take the pan from the freezer and use a fork to break up the solid bits and stir them back into the remaining liquid, crushing any larger pieces under the fork. Freeze for another 15 to 25 minutes or so, then stir the mixture with the fork as before. Continue this process until all of the liquid has frozen and the granité has a light, coarse-snow texture. This might take 1 to 1½ hours total. If you're not using the granité soon, scrape it into a freezer-proof, airtight container and freeze. The texture is best if served within 1 to 2 hours, but the flavor will hold for 4 to 5 days.

THE BRACING ACIDITY of grapefruit is one of my favorite counterpoints for oysters, here with a touch of extra aroma and flavor from fresh basil.

GRAPEFRUIT-BASIL GRANITÉ

+ In a small bowl, stir together the grapefruit juice, vinegar, basil, and sugar until the sugar is dissolved.

+ Freeze and stir the mixture (see Basic Freezing Technique, page 57).

+ To serve, take the granité from the freezer and scrape it again with a fork to loosen it. Top each oyster with some of the granité and serve right away (see the tips for serving raw oysters, page 48).

MAKES ABOUT 3 CUPS,
enough for 4 dozen half-shell oysters

1½ cups freshly squeezed pink grapefruit juice (from about 2 large or 3 medium grapefruit)

2 tablespoons red wine vinegar

1 tablespoon finely minced fresh basil

2 teaspoons sugar

SHISO IS A *spiky-edged, deep-green herb used in Japanese cuisine. A relative of mint, it has quite a different flavor, grassy-earthy with almost a touch of lemon. It can be hard to find in stores, but it makes a great garden herb if you have some space for it. You can use mint instead for equally refreshing results.*

CUCUMBER-SHISO GRANITÉ

**MAKES ABOUT
2½ CUPS,** *enough
for 3½ dozen half-
shell oysters*

1 small English
cucumber or medium
regular cucumber
(about 12 ounces)

3 tablespoons freshly
squeezed lime juice

2 tablespoons minced
fresh shiso

Kosher salt

✦ Trim and peel the cucumber (remove the seeds if not using English cucumber) and cut it into 1-inch pieces. Puree the cucumber in a food processor until a very smooth, juicy pulp is created. Add the lime juice, shiso, and a pinch of salt, and blend for another 30 seconds or so.

✦ Freeze and stir the mixture (see Basic Freezing Technique, page 57).

✦ To serve, take the granité from the freezer and scrape it again with a fork to loosen it. Top each oyster with some of the granité and serve right away (see the tips for serving raw oysters, page 48).

THIS RECIPE ECHOES elements from classic cocktail sauce, but it's a chunkier version for a more toothsome twist. Feel free to use a different pepper sauce than Tabasco; brands vary in intensity of heat, so adjust the amount used to suit your taste.

"COCKTAIL" RELISH

✦ In a small bowl, stir together the tomato, green onions, ketchup, lemon juice, horseradish, Tabasco, and a good pinch of salt. Let the relish sit for about 30 minutes, stirring occasionally, to allow the flavors to blend.

✦ Transfer the relish to a small ramekin or other small serving dish and refrigerate until ready to serve, up to 1 hour (see the tips for serving raw oysters, page 48).

MAKES ABOUT 1¼ CUPS,
enough for about
4½ dozen half-shell
oysters

1 cup finely chopped
    tomato

2 green onions, white
    and light-green
    parts minced

1 tablespoon ketchup

1 tablespoon freshly
    squeezed lemon juice

1 teaspoon prepared
    horseradish

½ teaspoon

Tabasco sauce

Kosher salt

KIMCHI—TRADITIONAL KOREAN FERMENTED vegetables, often cabbage— brings bold, spicy flavor to whatever context in which it's served. Its character is tempered a bit with a bright, crisp complement from cucumber. If you're a big fan of kimchi, feel free to amend the proportions, using a half cup each of the cucumber and kimchi. As is, this offers a milder kimchi flavor that most oyster slurpers should enjoy.

KIMCHI-CUCUMBER RELISH

✦ In a small bowl, stir together the cucumber, kimchi, rice vinegar, and soy sauce. Taste for seasoning, adding a bit more vinegar or soy sauce to taste. Let the relish sit for about 30 minutes, stirring occasionally, to allow the flavors to blend.

✦ Transfer the relish to a small ramekin or other small serving dish and refrigerate until ready to serve, up to 1 hour (see the tips for serving raw oysters, page 48).

MAKES 1 CUP, *enough for about 4 dozen half-shell oysters*

¾ cup peeled and seeded finely chopped cucumber

¼ cup finely chopped kimchi

1 teaspoon unseasoned rice vinegar, plus more to taste

¼ teaspoon soy sauce, plus more to taste (optional)

THIS OVER-TWENTY-ONE RELISH has some spirited character from aquavit, the traditional Scandinavian spirit infused with any from among a range of herbs and spices. Many bottles will at least hint at the ingredients that flavor their product; if you have a choice, lean toward those with fennel-dill-anise elements, though most aquavit should work fine here.

FENNEL-AQUAVIT RELISH

MAKES ABOUT 1¼ CUPS,
*enough for about
4½ dozen half-shell
oysters*

1 small fennel bulb, with
  green fronds if possible

¼ cup aquavit

Kosher salt

✦ Trim the fennel bulb (see note below), reserving the green fronds. Coarsely chop the bulb and pulse it in a food processor until finely chopped. You can finely chop the bulb by hand, if you prefer, but the agitation by the food processor blades helps draw some of the flavorful juices from the fennel.

✦ Chop enough of the fennel fronds to measure 1 to 2 tablespoons. In a small bowl, stir together the fennel bulb, fennel fronds, and aquavit with a pinch of salt. Let the relish sit for about 30 minutes, stirring occasionally, to allow the flavors to blend. Transfer the relish to a small ramekin or other small serving dish and refrigerate until ready to serve, up to 1 hour (see the tips for serving raw oysters, page 48).

PREPARING FENNEL BULB

Trim the stalks from the fennel at the point where they meet the bulb. Reserve the tender green fronds if needed in the recipe and discard the stalks (or save them for a batch of fish or vegetable stock). Cut away the tough base from the bulb and set the bulb upright on the cutting board. Halve it vertically, from the top toward the base. If the outer layer is quite thick and tough or bruised and blemished, discard it. Cut out the tough core from each half, then chop or slice the fennel as needed.

ONE OF THE world's great chilled soups is gazpacho, which comes in many forms but most often brings to mind the red tomato-based soup with crisp cucumber and aromatic character from garlic and herbs. Those flavors beautifully complement raw oysters, as it happens. The liquid portion, to which a splash of tequila is added, is a delicious bonus.

GAZPACHO RELISH WITH TEQUILA CHASER

+ In a food processor, combine the tomato, cucumber, cilantro, green onion, lime juice, oil, jalapeño, garlic, cumin, and a pinch of salt and pulse for 20 to 30 seconds until finely chopped and well blended, scraping down the sides of the bowl once or twice. There should still be a little texture; you don't want to make a smooth puree.

+ Spoon the mixture into a fine sieve set over a bowl and let sit for 15 to 20 minutes to drain off the flavorful liquid; stir now and then to help it drain evenly. You should have a generous ¼ cup or almost ½ cup of liquid. Add about the same amount of tequila as you have juice to the liquid and refrigerate until ready to serve. Spoon the relish into a small ramekin or other small serving dish and refrigerate until ready to serve, up to 1 hour. When serving, restir the chaser and serve a couple tablespoons each in shot glasses (see the tips for serving raw oysters, page 48).

MAKES 1 SCANT CUP RELISH, *enough for about 3½ dozen half-shell oysters and 6 to 8 chasers*

1 cup finely chopped tomato

½ cup peeled, seeded, and chopped cucumber

2 tablespoons chopped fresh cilantro

2 tablespoons chopped green onion, white and light-green parts

2 tablespoons freshly squeezed lime juice

2 tablespoons olive oil

2 teaspoons chopped jalapeño

½ teaspoon finely chopped garlic

Pinch ground cumin

Kosher salt

About ½ cup blanco or silver tequila

BAKED & GRILLED

THIS IS A VERSATILE recipe that can be served as a main course, appetizer, or cocktail bite from a platter. If you have spare rock salt on hand, you can form small mounds on the serving plates to help hold the oyster shells even.

BAKED OYSTERS WITH TENDER LEEKS & THYME

+ Set the oven rack in the center of the oven. Preheat the oven to 450 degrees F. Line a rimmed baking sheet with rock salt or cut a piece of aluminum foil twice as long as the baking sheet and crumple it on the surface of the pan.

+ Melt the butter in a medium skillet over medium heat. Add the leeks and cook, stirring often, until they begin to soften, 2 to 3 minutes. Stir in ¾ teaspoon of the thyme, ¼ teaspoon of the lemon zest, and a good pinch each of salt and pepper. Reduce the heat to medium, cover the skillet with its lid or a piece of aluminum foil, and cook, stirring occasionally, until the leeks are quite tender, 10 to 12 minutes longer. The leeks should not brown; reduce the heat if needed.

+ While the leeks are cooking, in a small bowl, stir together the bread crumbs and Parmesan with the remaining ¼ teaspoon thyme and ¼ teaspoon lemon zest. Set aside.

MAKES 2 MAIN COURSE SERVINGS *or 4 to 6 appetizer servings*

Rock salt, for baking

2 tablespoons unsalted butter

4 medium or 3 large leeks, trimmed and cleaned (see note on following page), white and light-green portions thinly sliced

1 teaspoon minced fresh thyme, divided

½ teaspoon finely grated lemon zest, divided

Kosher salt and freshly ground black pepper

¼ cup fine dried bread crumbs

(CONTINUED)

2 tablespoons finely
grated Parmesan
cheese

¼ cup dry white wine

12 medium to large
oysters in their shells,
shells well rinsed

+ Uncover the leeks, stir in the wine, and cook until the liquid has mostly evaporated, 1 to 2 minutes. Take the skillet from the heat and set aside to cool.

+ Shuck the oysters (see Shucking Oysters, page 31), discarding the top shell. Cut the adductor muscle from the bottom shell, leaving the oyster in place. A little oyster liquor is good, but pour off excess if there is quite a lot of liquor in some of the shells. Nestle the oysters into the rock salt or aluminum foil on the baking sheet so they sit evenly and securely. Top the oysters with the leek mixture, spreading it out a bit to cover the oysters. Sprinkle the bread crumb mixture evenly over the leeks.

+ Bake until the oysters are plump and the bread crumbs are nicely browned, 8 to 10 minutes. Use tongs or an oven mitt to transfer the oysters to individual plates or a platter, perching them as evenly as you're able. Serve right away.

CLEANING LEEKS

The thin layers of a leek can sometimes harbor grit, so it's best to clean them before using. First trim away the root end and the darker-green top portion, which is quite tough (though it can be used in a batch of stock). Then split the leek lengthwise and run cool water through the layers of the leek to draw off any grit. Pat it dry with a kitchen towel and use as directed.

THIS IS MY take on the barbecue sauce theme, which is a popular accent for grilled and baked oysters. So many barbecue sauces have a sweet element that I find clashes with oysters, so I go full-on savory with a bold, devilish flavor.

OYSTERS BAKED WITH DEVIL SAUCE

+ Set an oven rack about 5 inches below the top element. Preheat the oven to 450 degrees F. Line a rimmed baking sheet with rock salt or cut a piece of aluminum foil twice as long as the baking sheet and crumple it on the surface of the pan.

+ To make the sauce, heat the oil in a medium skillet over medium heat. Add the shallot and cook, stirring occasionally, until tender, 3 to 4 minutes. Add the vermouth and cook until the liquid has reduced by about half, 2 to 3 minutes. Take the pan from the heat and add the tomato paste, mustard, Worcestershire, Tabasco to taste, and a pinch of salt. Stir well to combine and let the sauce cool to room temperature.

MAKES 4 MAIN COURSE SERVINGS *or 8 to 12 appetizer servings*

Rock salt, for baking

FOR THE SAUCE:

1 tablespoon olive oil

¼ cup minced shallot or onion

½ cup dry vermouth

2 tablespoons tomato paste

1 tablespoon Dijon mustard

2 teaspoons Worcestershire sauce

About 1 teaspoon Tabasco or other hot sauce, plus more or less to taste

Kosher salt

~~~~~~~~

24 medium oysters in their shells, shells well rinsed

(CONTINUED)

✦ Shuck the oysters (see Shucking Oysters, page 31), discarding the top shell. Cut the adductor muscle from the bottom shell, leaving the oyster in place. A little oyster liquor is good, but pour off excess if there is quite a lot of liquor in some of the shells. Nestle the oysters into the rock salt or aluminum foil on the baking sheet so they sit evenly and securely. Top the oysters with the sauce, about ½ teaspoon each, and bake until the oysters are plump and juices around the edge are bubbling, 8 to 10 minutes. Use tongs or an oven mitt to transfer the oysters to individual plates or a platter, perching them as evenly as you're able. Serve right away.

LOOK FOR PREPARED puff pastry in the freezer section of your grocery store. If you can find all-butter puff pastry (which might mean hitting a specialty shop or gourmet grocery), the flavor really is best. Because different producers make puff pastry sheets in different sizes, you might need to amend the size and shape of yours a bit. Be sure to plan ahead, as the frozen pastry needs to thaw completely before you use it.

GREEN CURRY OYSTER & SPINACH PUFFS

MAKES 32 PUFFS

8 to 10 ounces jarred small to medium oysters, drained

2 tablespoons unsalted butter

½ cup minced onion

2 tablespoons prepared green curry paste

4 packed cups washed fresh spinach (about 4½ ounces or 1 small bunch), coarsely chopped, or half of 1 (10-ounce) package frozen chopped spinach, thawed, excess liquid squeezed out

Kosher salt and freshly ground black pepper

About 1 pound puff pastry, thawed

+ Set 2 oven racks at the centermost positions. Preheat the oven to 425 degrees F. Line 2 baking sheets with parchment paper or silicone baking mats.

+ Coarsely chop the oysters and lay them on paper towels to draw off excess moisture, which will help keep the pastry from becoming soggy.

+ Heat the butter in a medium skillet over medium heat. When the butter has melted, add the onion and cook, stirring occasionally, until aromatic but not browned, 1 to 2 minutes. Stir in the curry paste to evenly blend with the onion. Add about half of the spinach and cook, stirring, until mostly wilted, then add the remaining spinach. Continue cooking until the spinach is evenly tender and bright green, and any excess moisture has cooked off, 3 to 4 minutes longer. (If using thawed frozen spinach, add it to the pan all at once and cook for a few minutes until well blended with the onion.) Season to taste with salt and pepper.

(CONTINUED)

+ Transfer the spinach mixture to a medium bowl and let cool. When cooled, stir in the oysters.

+ Unfold half of the puff pastry onto a lightly floured work surface. Roll it out a bit so that the dough is roughly 12 by 12 inches and about ⅛ inch thick. (Other dimensions are okay, depending on the shape of the sheet you begin with, but the final lengths of the sides should be divisible by 3 inches.) Cut the dough into 3-inch squares, preferably using the rolling blade of a pastry or pizza cutter.

+ Spoon about 1 teaspoon of the oyster mixture just off-center onto a pastry square and flatten it a bit. Very lightly brush the pastry edges with water and fold one corner over to meet its opposite side, forming a triangle. Press the edges well with your fingers to seal, set the triangle on one of the prepared baking sheets, and continue forming triangles with the remaining ingredients.

+ Use kitchen shears or the tip of a small knife to snip a small vent in the top of each pastry triangle. Bake until the pastry is well puffed and moderately browned, 15 to 18 minutes, switching the baking sheets halfway for even baking. Let the pastries cool for about 5 minutes before transferring the puffs to a platter or plates for serving.

SCALLOPED OYSTERS IS one of those classic recipes that is easy to make and richly satisfying. How could it be otherwise with oysters, bread crumbs, cream, and butter all baked together? This is an update on that idea, adding some flavorful kale and a delightful crunch from a topping of buttery bread crumbs. Either regular curly kale or lacinato kale can be used; the latter may take an extra minute or two to wilt.

This makes a great wintry main course, perhaps with roasted or braised root vegetables alongside. It can be served as an appetizer as well.

OYSTER & KALE GRATIN WITH BROWN-BUTTER CRUMBS

+ Preheat the oven to 400 degrees F. Butter a 12-inch gratin dish or similar shallow baking dish.

+ Stack 4 or 5 of the kale leaves at a time and cut across them into strips 1 to 2 inches wide.

+ Melt 2 tablespoons of the butter in a large skillet over medium heat. Add the shallot and cook, stirring occasionally, until tender, 3 to 4 minutes. Add a couple handfuls of the kale and cook, stirring, until it is about half wilted, then add another handful of kale. Continue adding the kale in batches as room becomes available in the skillet. The kale does not need to become fully tender, just evenly wilted; this should take about 8 to 10 minutes total.

MAKES 4 MAIN COURSE SERVINGS *or 8 appetizer servings*

6 tablespoons unsalted butter, divided, plus more for buttering

2 bunches kale (about 12 ounces each), tough stems removed

1 large shallot, thinly sliced (about ¾ cup)

½ cup freshly grated Parmesan cheese (about 2 ounces)

(CONTINUED)

+ Arrange the kale and shallot mixture in an even layer in the gratin dish. Sprinkle the Parmesan over the kale and season with pepper to taste. In a small bowl, stir together the half-and-half with 3 to 4 tablespoons of the oyster liquor. Pour all but ½ cup of the mixture over the kale. Bake until the kale is tender, the cheese is just beginning to brown, and the liquids bubble around the edges, 15 to 20 minutes.

+ While the kale is baking, melt the remaining 4 tablespoons butter in a medium skillet over medium heat. After the butter has melted, continue cooking until the milk solids have turned a medium brown and the butter smells slightly nutty, 2 to 3 minutes longer. Take the skillet from the heat, add the bread crumbs, and stir until evenly blended.

+ Take the gratin dish from the oven. Arrange the oysters evenly over the kale and drizzle them with the reserved half-and-half mixture. Scatter the bread crumbs evenly over the oysters and return the gratin dish to the oven to bake until the oysters are plump and the bread crumbs are nicely browned, 8 to 10 minutes. Let the gratin sit for a few minutes before serving.

Freshly ground black pepper

1½ cups half-and-half, plus more if needed

20 to 24 jarred small to medium oysters, with their liquor

½ cup fine dried bread crumbs

THESE OYSTERS ARE a wonderful snack as-is for cocktail hour on small crackers, or use them in the Crostini with Smoked Oysters (page 80). You could toss them with pasta, add some to a potato salad, or add a bit of smoky character to one of the soups (as an accent, not instead of the fresh oysters). There are plenty of possibilities.

Oysters being so much smaller than, say, a brisket or other large pieces of meat typically smoked, be sure to check if your grill grate has a fine enough grid to securely hold the shucked oysters. If not, use a grilling rack. Those intended for grilling vegetables are ideal, allowing smoke contact from both sides. Or you could use a large metal cooling rack that has a fine, crosshatch grid, though you might want to commit it to future grilling/smoking projects rather than expecting to use it again to cool a batch of sugar cookies.

If you have a smoker, of course this is an ideal time to use it, following the manufacturer's instructions. Your total smoke time may vary, based on the level of heat and distance the oysters are from the heat source.

ALDER SMOKED OYSTERS

**MAKES 36
SMOKED OYSTERS**

FOR THE BRINE:

3 cups warm water

¼ cup kosher salt

3 tablespoons packed
light brown sugar

1 tablespoon minced or
pressed garlic

1 tablespoon finely grated
peeled fresh ginger

½ teaspoon freshly
ground black pepper

✦ To make the brine, in a large bowl, stir together the water, salt, sugar, garlic, ginger, and pepper until the salt and sugar have dissolved. Let the brine cool to room temperature.

✦ Add the oysters to the cooled brine. They should be fully covered; add a bit more cold water if needed. Cover and refrigerate the oysters for 1 to 3 hours.

✦ When ready to smoke the oysters, prepare an outdoor grill for indirect heat. If you have temperature control, 225 to 250 degrees F is about right. Soak the wood chips in cool water for at least 30 minutes. Lightly oil the grilling rack.

+ Drain the oysters from the brine, rinse them lightly under cold water, and dry them on paper towels. Arrange the oysters on the grilling rack; they can be close but should be touching each other as little as possible.

+ Half fill a small aluminum pan with water and put it between the coal piles in your charcoal grill or to one side of a gas grill. Drain the wood chips and scatter about half of them over the coals or put them in your grill's smoker box.

+ Set the rack with the oysters on the grill, away from the heat source. Quickly cover the grill to retain the maximum heat and smoke. Smoke the oysters until they are firm and nicely bronzed, 1½ to 2 hours (internal temperature should read 145 degrees F for 15 seconds, measured using an instant-read thermometer). Replenish with a few wood chips as needed, and add a few more charcoal pieces every 30 minutes or so.

+ Take the grilling rack from the grate and let the oysters cool. If not serving right away, store the oysters in an airtight container and refrigerate for up to 3 days.

36 freshly shucked medium to large oysters (see Shucking Oysters, page 31) or jarred small to medium oysters, drained

2 cups alder or apple wood chips

AS A KID I'd happily snack on smoked oysters plopped on whatever type of cracker was at hand. From that simple starting point, I dress things up a bit with a couple of my favorite ingredients: lemons and chickpeas. This is a perfect cocktail hour nibble or game-night snack. Look for small-batch smoked oysters from regional companies, such as Ekone Oyster Company, on Willapa Bay in Washington (see Oyster Shopping Guide, page 135). Better yet: smoke your own (see Alder Smoked Oysters, page 78).

CROSTINI WITH SMOKED OYSTERS

MAKES 18 CROSTINI

3 tablespoons olive oil, divided, plus more if needed

½ cup finely chopped onion

1 (14-ounce) can chickpeas, drained and rinsed

⅓ cup freshly squeezed lemon juice, plus more if needed

2 teaspoons finely grated lemon zest

Kosher salt and freshly ground black pepper

18 smoked oysters (about 4 to 5 ounces), at room temperature

18 slices baguette, lightly toasted

✦ Heat 2 tablespoons of the oil in a medium saucepan over medium heat. Add the onion and cook, stirring occasionally, until tender and aromatic, 3 to 4 minutes. Add the chickpeas, lemon juice, and lemon zest with a good pinch each of salt and pepper. Cook, stirring occasionally, until the chickpeas have softened a bit, 5 to 7 minutes.

✦ Take the pan from the heat, add the remaining 1 tablespoon oil, and use a potato masher or sturdy whisk to mash the chickpeas to a texture that's cohesive and spreadable but still a bit chunky. Taste for seasoning, adding salt, pepper, or a bit more lemon juice if needed. The chickpea mixture can be made up to 1 day in advance and refrigerated, covered. Allow the chickpea mixture to come to room temperature before serving. You may need to add a tablespoon or two of water to return it to a spreadable consistency.

✦ To serve, spread a generous tablespoon of the smashed chickpeas onto the toasted bread. Top each slice with a smoked oyster and arrange the crostini on a platter.

HOW TO SERVE GRILLED OYSTERS

When grilling oysters, be sure you're starting with cleaned, shut-tight oysters. Avoid choosing very small oysters for grilling; they may be harder to manage on the grill and tend to be prime for slurping anyway.

You have two options: grilling the oysters preshucked on the half shell or whole in their shells. The benefits of preshucked include more even cooking, you can easily tell when they're done, a sauce or topping can be added before grilling so it melds more with oysters as they cook, and all the work's done in advance. Once grilled, just eat! The con arguments for preshucking include the extra step of shucking, plus the fact that, if the shells aren't perched evenly, toppings or sauces risk dripping out of shells during cooking and when transferred from the grill.

For cooking the oysters whole in their shells, just set them on the grill; no further preparation is required. The trick here is that some oysters will tell you when they're ready by popping their shells, others won't, leaving you to guess when to pull them off and risking that some get a little overcooked. Also, the sauces or toppings are more of an add-on accent rather than mingled with the oysters while cooking. And you likely still need to do a bit of shucking to open some, though less than preshucking requires. Note that on occasion you may get an oyster that explodes a bit from the heat, so using the grill lid with in-shell oysters is recommended.

Both methods are good; it's your choice. Either way, start with a grill that's preheated for direct medium-high heat. Total grill time will vary with different styles of grill, temperature, size of oysters, and whether the grill is covered or not.

PRESHUCK GRILL METHOD

Shuck the oysters (see Shucking Oysters, page 31) and sever the lower adductor muscle. Drain off some of the liquor from each shell so the oyster is moist but not swimming; this helps avoid diluting the sauces during cooking, but if you're cooking the oysters au naturel you can leave all the liquor. Top the oysters with one of the sauces that follow (pages 85 to 87). (You can do so up to an hour ahead, keeping the oysters chilled on rimmed trays until they're ready to grill.) Use long-handled tongs to set the oysters on the preheated grill, perching the shells as evenly as you're able. Grill until the oysters are plump, their edges have curled, and juices around the edge are bubbling, about five to seven minutes. Use the tongs to transfer the oysters to a platter or individual plates for serving, alerting guests to wait a few minutes before diving in.

GRILL WHOLE METHOD

Set the whole cleaned oysters directly on the preheated grill, cupped-side down, perching the shells as evenly as you're able. Grill, covered, until the shells have popped a bit or you see active bubbling around the edges of the shells, five to ten minutes, perhaps a few minutes longer for larger oysters and/or thicker shells. Use long-handled tongs to transfer the opened oysters to a tray, and when cool enough to handle, use a shucking knife to remove the top shell and to sever the lower adductor muscle in each oyster, if needed. Top with one of the sauces that follow.

BAKING OYSTERS

Baking oysters in their shells is a great all-weather variant on out-door grilling. Set the cleaned oysters cupped-side down on a rimmed baking sheet or large roasting pan or baking dish. Bake in a 425-degree-F oven until the oysters pop open a bit, or until you see liquids actively bubbling around the edges of the shells, indicating they should be good to go. This might take eight to twelve minutes depending on the size and shell thickness of the oysters; in the dry heat of the oven you want to avoid overcooking or the oyster meat will dry up quite a lot. Any oysters that don't open may need a bit of shucking help, or you can also preshuck and bake if you prefer.

IT'S FUN TO play around with the basic premise of pesto using different greens and nuts, sometimes with garlic and/or Parmesan cheese, sometimes without, depending on how it will be used. In this recipe the peppery character of arugula is a delicious contrast to the rich oysters, and the vivid green makes a striking presentation to boot.

ARUGULA-ALMOND PESTO

✦ Put the garlic clove in a food processor and pulse a few times to finely chop, scraping down the sides once or twice. Add the arugula, almonds, and oil with a good pinch each of salt and pepper. Puree until smooth, scraping down the sides as needed. The pesto should be on the thick side, but spread out a bit when scooped up in a spoon. Add a dash more oil or a bit of water if needed. If making the pesto in advance, you can cover and refrigerate it for up to 24 hours, but allow it to come to room temperature before serving (see the oyster grilling tips on page 81).

MAKES ABOUT ¾ CUP, *enough for about 3 dozen grilled oysters*

1 clove garlic

2 cups moderately packed arugula (about 2 ounces)

½ cup slivered almonds

¼ cup olive oil, plus more if needed

Kosher salt and freshly ground black pepper

THE MEATY CHARACTER of this relish makes the oysters taste extra substantial, almost burger-like. This relish would be a particularly good choice for a main-course grilled option, with a crisp coleslaw alongside. A teaspoon or so of finely chopped chipotle chiles en adobo can add another level of robust and spicy flavor if you like.

SMOKEY TOMATO-BACON RELISH

MAKES 1 SCANT CUP,
*enough for about
2½ dozen grilled oysters*

4 strips thick-cut smoked
  bacon, cut lengthwise
  in half and across
  into ¼-inch pieces

¼ cup finely chopped
  shallot or onion

1 cup finely chopped
  tomato

Kosher salt and freshly
  ground black pepper

✦ Cook the bacon in a medium skillet over medium heat, stirring often, until most of the fat has rendered and the bacon is lightly browned, 5 to 7 minutes. If there looks to be more than about 1 tablespoon of fat, pour the excess off (it can be saved for another use), then add the shallot and cook until tender and aromatic, about 2 minutes. Stir in the tomato and cook until it has softened, the excess liquid has evaporated, and the mixture has thickened slightly, 3 to 4 minutes. Season to taste with salt and pepper and set aside until ready to serve. If making the relish in advance, you can cover and refrigerate it for up to 6 hours, but allow it to come to room temperature before serving (see the oyster grilling tips on page 81).

GARLIC BUTTER ON grilled oysters is one of life's simple pleasures. I ramp up the flavor a bit here using fresh sage. Flat-leaf parsley or chives would be delicious here too, or consider a combination of all three.

GARLIC-SAGE BUTTER

✦ In a small bowl, combine the butter, sage, and garlic with a good pinch of salt. Stir together with a fork, mashing and stirring well to be sure the mixture is evenly blended. If not grilling the oysters for 1 hour or more, refrigerate the butter, which can be made up to 2 days in advance. Allow the butter to soften at room temperature before using (see the oyster grilling tips on page 81).

> NOTE: The butter is used as is if you are shucking the oysters before grilling. If you are cooking the oysters whole in their shells, the seasoned butter should be melted and drizzled over the cooked oysters just before serving.

MAKES ABOUT ½ CUP, *enough for about 2 dozen grilled oysters*

½ cup unsalted butter, at room temperature

1 tablespoon finely minced fresh sage

1 teaspoon minced or pressed garlic

Kosher salt

FRIED & SAUTÉED

THIS IS ONE of the most popular ways to cook oysters: oysters, some seasoned flour, and a bit of fat (butter, oil, bacon fat, you choose) are all you need. For a gluten-free variation, you can use other types of flour such as chickpea or rice. You may need a bit extra in order to fully coat the oysters, as not all flours coat the same.

In a pinch, any delicious tartar sauce will be a fine complement, but the savory crunch of this fennel version is worth the few extra minutes to whip it together. Not all fennel bulbs come with tender green fronds still attached, but try to find a bulb that does. The greens make a nice herbal accent in the tartar sauce. If you've got fronds to spare, scatter them—whole or just coarsely chopped—over the oysters just before serving.

PAN-FRIED OYSTERS
WITH FENNEL TARTAR SAUCE

✦ To make the tartar sauce, combine the mayonnaise, fennel bulb, cornichon, fennel fronds, and vinegar and stir well to blend. Season to taste with salt and pepper and refrigerate until ready to serve, preferably for at least 1 hour in advance to allow the flavors to blend.

✦ Preheat the oven to 200 degrees F. Line a rimmed baking sheet with brown paper or paper towels and set an oblong wire rack on top, if you have one. Lightly flour another baking sheet or a tray for holding the coated oysters.

✦ On a large plate or in a shallow bowl, stir together the flour, salt, and pepper. Add a few of the oysters at a time, tossing well to evenly coat with the flour mixture, then lift them out and shake off the excess flour. Set the coated oysters aside on the floured

MAKES 2 MAIN COURSE SERVINGS *or 4 to 6 appetizer servings*

FOR THE FENNEL TARTAR SAUCE:

¾ cup mayonnaise

½ cup finely chopped fennel bulb (see note, page 64)

3 tablespoons finely chopped cornichon or dill pickle

2 tablespoons chopped fennel fronds or minced chives

(CONTINUED)

1 tablespoon white wine vinegar or freshly squeezed lemon juice, plus more if needed

Kosher salt and freshly ground black pepper

~~~~~~~~~~

¾ cup unbleached all-purpose flour, plus more for flouring

½ teaspoon kosher salt

¼ teaspoon freshly ground black pepper

24 freshly shucked medium oysters (see Shucking Oysters, page 31) or jarred small oysters, drained

Mild olive oil or vegetable oil, for frying

baking sheet and continue coating the remaining oysters. Reserve the excess flour.

+ Heat about ¼ inch of oil in a large heavy skillet, such as cast iron, over medium heat. Keep in mind that the heavier the pan, the longer it will take to preheat.

+ While the pan is heating, quickly retoss the oysters 3 or 4 at a time in the flour to ensure an even coating. When the oil is hot, carefully add about 6 of the oysters (don't crowd the pan; cook fewer if needed) and cook until nicely browned, about 3 minutes. Turn the oysters and brown on the other side, 2 to 3 minutes longer. Transfer the oysters to the prepared baking sheet and keep them warm in the oven while frying the remaining oysters. Add a bit more oil to the pan and allow the oil to reheat if needed between batches.

+ Taste the tartar sauce again just before serving, adjusting the seasoning if needed. Arrange the oysters on individual plates with a generous spoonful of the sauce alongside and serve right away.

A RIFF ON the New Orleans po'boy, Asian character comes through with the Japanese spice blend shichimi togarashi, *which often includes red pepper flakes, dried orange peel, dried seaweed, and sesame seeds. Keep the oysters in their briny liquor until just before coating in the crumbs, for just the right amount of moisture for the panko to cling to.*

OYSTER SLIDERS WITH TOGARASHI SLAW

MAKES 12 SLIDERS

FOR THE TOGARASHI SLAW:

¾ cup mayonnaise

⅓ cup finely chopped green onion

Kosher salt

½ medium cucumber (about 6 ounces), peeled and seeded

1 bunch radishes (about 8 ounces), trimmed

1 medium carrot, trimmed, peeled, and cut into about 2 ½-inch lengths

1 cup moderately packed finely shredded Napa or savoy cabbage

2 tablespoons unseasoned rice vinegar

¾ teaspoon toasted sesame oil

½ teaspoon *shichimi togarashi*

✦ To make the slaw, in a medium bowl, stir together the mayonnaise, green onion, and a pinch of salt. Set aside.

✦ Use a food processor with the grater plate or the large holes of a box grater to grate the cucumber. Squeeze the excess liquid from the cucumber and put it in a large bowl. Grate the radishes and carrot and add them, along with the cabbage, to the cucumber. Add about ⅓ cup of the mayonnaise mixture (reserving the rest as a spread for the buns), the rice vinegar, sesame oil, and *shichimi togarashi*, and toss well to mix. The vegetables should be just lightly coated.

✦ Set aside while preparing the oysters, stirring the slaw occasionally. (If making the slaw more than 1 hour in advance, cover the bowl and refrigerate, along with the remaining mayonnaise mixture, allowing it to come to room temperature before serving; note that the vegetables will lose some of their crunch and the slaw will become wetter the longer it sits.)

(CONTINUED)

+ Preheat the oven to 200 degrees F. Line a rimmed baking sheet with brown paper or paper towels and set an oblong wire rack on top, if you have one. Scatter about ½ cup of the panko in another rimmed baking sheet or tray for holding the coated oysters.

+ Heat about ¼ inch of oil in a large heavy skillet, such as cast iron, over medium heat. Keep in mind that the heavier the pan, the longer it will take to preheat.

+ Spread the remaining 1½ cups panko on a plate. Add a couple of oysters to the panko, scatter some of the panko over the oysters, and press gently to help the crumbs adhere. Set the oysters aside on the crumb-covered tray and continue coating the remaining oysters. Let the oysters sit for about 5 minutes, then lightly coat them once more to be sure they're evenly covered.

+ Add half of the oysters to the skillet (don't crowd the pan; cook fewer if needed) and fry until nicely browned, about 3 minutes. Carefully turn the oysters and fry on the other side, 2 to 3 minutes longer. Transfer the oysters to the prepared baking sheet and keep them warm in the oven while frying the remaining oysters.

+ Halve the buns if they're not already split. Spread the remaining mayonnaise mixture on the bottom half of the buns. Taste the slaw for seasoning, adding more salt or *shichimi togarashi* to taste. Spoon the slaw onto the buns and top with the oysters. Cap off the sandwiches with the top buns and serve right away, with any remaining slaw alongside.

2 cups panko bread crumbs, divided

Mild olive oil or vegetable oil, for frying

12 freshly shucked small to medium oysters (see Shucking Oysters, page 31) or jarred extra-small to small oysters, with their liquor

12 slider buns

NOTE: You can also serve the oysters and slaw on larger single-serving hoagies or other sandwich rolls. Or skip the bread and serve the fried oysters on the slaw in cleaned oyster shells or Asian soup spoons for cocktail party fare.

OKONOMIYAKI *IS ONE* of those dishes that is as much an idea as a recipe; there are a great many variations on ingredients used and how the recipe is composed. My favorite is Osaka style, ingredients blended first in a batter and cooked together. The pancake should be not too thick, so that it cooks evenly. This makes an ideal snack or first course.

This recipe makes two medium pancakes that are easier to cook than one large one, particularly when it comes to flipping. You can make this as one larger pancake instead, cooking each side one to two minutes longer, though flipping gets trickier.

OYSTER OKONOMIYAKI (SAVORY JAPANESE PANCAKE)

MAKES 4 TO 6 APPETIZER SERVINGS

FOR THE SAUCE:

2 tablespoons mayonnaise

1 teaspoon Worcestershire sauce

1 teaspoon mirin

1 teaspoon soy sauce

¾ cup unbleached all-purpose flour

½ cup water

+ To make the sauce, stir together the mayonnaise, Worcestershire, mirin, and soy sauce. Set aside.

+ Preheat a large skillet, preferably nonstick, over medium heat. Preheat the oven to 200 degrees F.

+ While the skillet is heating, make the batter. Put the flour in a large bowl and whisk in the water, oyster liquor, and salt until smooth and well blended. If the oysters you're using are on the bigger side, you may want to cut each in half. Whisk the eggs into the batter, then add the oysters, cabbage, mushrooms.

+ Set aside about 2 tablespoons of the dark-green portion of the green onions for garnish, and add the remaining amount to the batter. Stir gently to thoroughly blend.

- ✦ When the skillet is heated, add 1½ teaspoons of the oil and gently swirl the pan to evenly coat the bottom. Restir the pancake mixture, then add half of it to the skillet, doing your best to distribute the oysters evenly. Spread the mixture out and press gently to form an even layer. Cook until the pancake is nicely browned on the bottom and looks dry on the surface, 6 to 7 minutes. Use your largest spatula to carefully flip the pancake and cook until the other side browns and the vegetables are fully tender, 6 to 7 minutes longer. (If the pancake breaks up a bit when flipping, don't fret, simply reform and reshape it as best you can; it'll still taste fantastic.) Transfer the pancake to a baking sheet and keep it warm in the oven while cooking the second pancake in the same way, adding the remaining 1½ teaspoons oil to the skillet and stirring the pancake mixture again before adding it to the skillet.

- ✦ Gently slide both *okonomiyaki* onto a chopping board. Restir the sauce to mix and drizzle it over the pancakes. Scatter the reserved green onions over, then the bonito flakes. Cut each *okonomiyaki* into 6 wedges and serve.

12 freshly shucked extra-small to small oysters (see Shucking Oysters, page 31) or jarred yearling to extra-small oysters, plus ¼ cup liquor (if less liquor is available, add water to make ¼ cup)

½ teaspoon kosher salt

2 large eggs

1½ cups moderately packed finely shredded green cabbage

1½ cups thinly sliced shiitake mushrooms (about 3 ounces)

4 large or 6 small green onions, trimmed and thinly sliced at an angle

3 teaspoons mild olive or vegetable oil, divided

Bonito flakes or *furikake*, for serving (optional) (see note)

NOTE: Bonito flakes are whisper-thin slices of dried tuna and are a common garnish for *okonomiyaki*; when they hit the warm pancake the heat makes the flakes flutter a bit, quite dramatic! If you're unable to find bonito flakes, some types of *furikake* (a Japanese rice seasoning blend) include bonito flakes and that seasoning combination is quite good on the pancake as well. You can also skip this extra dash of garnish altogether.

THERE ARE A LOT of delicious complementary things going on in this salad: tender and crunchy, earthy and briny, fresh and bitter. You can prepare the greens and dressing and coat the oysters up to an hour in advance, refrigerating the greens and oysters. The greens should be dressed and the oysters cooked just before serving. If you don't have hazelnut oil on hand, you can simply use more of the olive oil for the dressing. As a variation you could swap out the radicchio and use four ounces of arugula instead. Whether using jarred or just-shucked oysters, keep them in their briny liquor until just before coating in the bread crumbs, as it will offer just the right amount of moisture for the crumbs to cling to.

ENDIVE & RADICCHIO SALAD WITH FRIED OYSTERS & HAZELNUTS

+ Preheat the oven to 200 degrees F. Line a rimmed baking sheet with brown paper or paper towels and set an oblong wire rack on top, if you have one.

+ Trim the stem ends from the endive and discard any blemished outer leaves. Cut each endive in half lengthwise and cut away the triangular core from the base. Cut across each half into roughly ¾-inch pieces. Put the endive in a large bowl.

+ Halve the radicchio and cut away the tough core. Discard any blemished outer leaves. Cut across each half into slices about ¼ inch thick and add them to the bowl with the endive. Cover with a damp kitchen towel or paper towels and set aside.

+ Put ½ cup of the hazelnuts in a food processor and pulse until finely ground (take care not to overgrind

MAKES 2 TO 3 MAIN COURSE SERVINGS *or 6 appetizer servings*

4 large heads Belgian endive (about ¾ pound)

1 small head radicchio (about 8 ounces)

1 cup hazelnuts (about 4 ounces), lightly toasted and skinned, divided

¾ cup fine dried bread crumbs

Kosher salt and freshly ground black pepper

3 tablespoons red wine vinegar

1 teaspoon Dijon mustard

(CONTINUED)

¼ cup mild olive oil, plus more for frying

2 tablespoons hazelnut oil (optional)

18 freshly shucked small to medium oysters (see Shucking Oysters, page 31) or jarred extra-small to small oysters, with their liquor

or you might end up with hazelnut butter). Add the bread crumbs and a good pinch each of salt and pepper, and pulse a few times to blend. Transfer the mixture to a plate. Coarsely chop the remaining ½ cup hazelnuts.

+ In a small bowl, whisk together the vinegar and mustard with a good pinch each of salt and pepper. While whisking, drizzle in the olive and hazelnut oils.

+ Heat about ¼ inch of olive oil in a large heavy skillet, such as cast iron, over medium heat. Keep in mind that the heavier the pan, the longer it will take to preheat.

+ While the oil is heating, toss 2 or 3 oysters at a time in the nut-crumb mixture, coating each oyster well and patting to remove excess. When the oil is heated, carefully add about 6 of the oysters (don't crowd the pan; cook fewer if needed) and cook until nicely browned, about 3 minutes. Turn the oysters and brown on the second side, 2 to 3 minutes longer. Transfer the oysters to the prepared baking sheet and keep them warm in the oven while frying the remaining oysters. Add a bit more oil to the pan and allow it to reheat if needed between batches.

+ Rewhisk the dressing to mix, then pour it over the endive and radicchio and toss well to evenly coat. Arrange the salad on individual plates and top with the oysters. Sprinkle with the remaining ½ cup hazelnuts and serve right away.

THESE OYSTERS GET a triple-dip, so the cracker coating has extra-crispy results. This retro style of pan-fried oysters could be served with good ol' tartar sauce (like my fennel version on page 91) or cocktail sauce (the relish on page 61 would be a great option). But this simple cream sauce, essentially a savory whipped cream seasoned with fresh dill, offers something a bit different.

CRACKER-COATED OYSTERS WITH DILLED CREAM

✦ Preheat the oven to 200 degrees F. Line a rimmed baking sheet with brown paper or paper towels and set an oblong wire rack on top, if you have one. Lightly flour another baking sheet or a tray for holding the coated oysters.

✦ On a large plate, put the flour with a generous pinch each of salt and pepper and stir to combine. Put the milk in a shallow bowl. Put the cracker crumbs on another large plate.

✦ Toss a few of the oysters in the flour until evenly coated (see The Wet and the Dry, page 103). Pat to remove excess flour, then add the oysters to the milk and gently turn to evenly moisten. Lift the oysters, allowing excess milk to drip off, then coat them well in the cracker crumbs. Set the coated oysters on the floured baking sheet and continue

MAKES 2 MAIN COURSE SERVINGS *or 4 to 6 appetizer servings*

¾ cup unbleached all-purpose flour, plus more for flouring

Kosher salt and freshly ground black pepper

½ cup whole or 2 percent milk

1½ cups finely crushed crackers (about 4 ounces or one sleeve), such as saltines or Ritz (see note on following page)

24 freshly shucked medium oysters (see Shucking Oysters, page 31) or jarred small oysters, with their liquor

(CONTINUED)

Mild olive or vegetable oil,
for frying

½ cup heavy cream

1 tablespoon minced
fresh dill

NOTE: For the cracker coating, roughly crush the crackers with your hands, then pulse in a food processor or put in a heavy plastic bag and crush with a rolling pin to form fine crumbs. Don't over-process; the crumbs should still have some texture, not be too fine.

coating the remaining oysters. Let the oysters sit for about 10 minutes so the coating sets. (The oysters can be coated up to 1 hour in advance and refrigerated until ready to cook.)

✦ Heat about ¼ inch of oil in a large heavy skillet, such as cast iron, over medium heat. Keep in mind that the heavier the pan, the longer it will take to preheat.

✦ While the oysters are sitting and the oil is heating, whip the cream in a medium bowl until medium peaks form. Whisk in about 2 tablespoons of oyster liquor, if you have some, then add the dill and a pinch of salt and continue whipping until the cream is well thickened. Set aside. (If the kitchen is quite warm, you can put the cream in the refrigerator, but it should ideally be room temperature when served.)

✦ When the oil is heated, carefully add about 6 of the oysters (don't crowd the pan; cook fewer if needed) and cook until nicely browned, about 3 minutes. Turn the oysters and brown on the second side, 2 to 3 minutes longer. Transfer the oysters to the prepared baking sheet and keep them warm in the oven while frying the remaining oysters. Add a bit more oil to the pan and allow it to reheat if needed between batches.

✦ Arrange the fried oysters on individual plates, add a generous dollop of the dilled cream alongside, and serve right away.

THE WET AND THE DRY

This goes for any time a recipe has you coating food in a succession of dry and wet ingredients. If you're not careful, in a matter of minutes your fingertips will be heavily coated, which not only limits your dexterity with gloppy fingers, but also wastes some of your coating ingredients. The trick is to devote one hand to dry elements (patting flour, moving to milk, patting crumbs, moving to tray) and devote the other to wet elements (oysters into flour, coating in milk and/or egg, and moving to crackers). The wet fingers stay wet, the dry ingredients stay dry, and you avoid the gooey combo altogether.

THIS IS A VARIANT on Hangtown fry, which is essentially an omelet or frittata made with fried oysters and bacon. Here oysters, bacon, potato, and onion are combined in a flavorful hash on which to perch a fried egg—or poached or scrambled, whatever suits your fancy. Just add fruit, coffee, and maybe a piece of toast for brunch. For a breakfast-for-dinner option, this recipe will serve two as a main course.

HANGTOWN HASH WITH FRIED EGGS

✦ Preheat the oven to 200 degrees F.

✦ If some of the oysters you're using are on the large side, cut them in half or quarters. Small oysters will be fine left whole.

✦ Cook the bacon in a large ovenproof skillet, preferably nonstick, over medium heat until lightly browned and most of the fat has rendered, 3 to 5 minutes. Scoop out the bacon to a plate and set aside. Pour off all but about 2 tablespoons of the bacon fat; the rest can be saved for another use.

✦ Reheat the skillet over medium heat and add the onion. Cook, stirring, until the onion begins to soften, 3 to 5 minutes. Add the potatoes and a good pinch each of salt and pepper and toss to combine. Cover the skillet, reduce the heat to medium-low, and cook, stirring occasionally, until the potatoes are nearly tender, about 10 minutes. Remove the lid and continue cooking until the potatoes are tender and lightly browned, 5 to 7 minutes longer.

MAKES 4 SERVINGS

12 to 18 freshly shucked small to medium oysters (see Shucking Oysters, page 31) or jarred extra-small to small oysters, drained

4 strips thick-cut bacon, cut across into ½-inch pieces

1 medium onion, finely chopped

3 medium Yukon Gold or other waxy potatoes, scrubbed and cut into ¼-inch dice

Kosher salt and freshly ground black pepper

¼ cup chopped fresh flat-leaf parsley

2 tablespoons chopped fresh chives

2 tablespoons unsalted butter

4 large eggs

(CONTINUED)

+ Add the oysters and increase the heat to medium. Cook, stirring gently but frequently, until the oysters are plump and their edges curl, 3 to 4 minutes. Take the skillet from the heat and stir in the bacon, parsley, and chives. Taste the hash for seasoning, adding more salt or pepper to taste, and set the skillet in the oven to keep the hash warm until ready to serve. (If you don't have a griddle or another large skillet for cooking the eggs, transfer the hash to a baking dish to keep it warm in the oven and wash the skillet before continuing.)

+ Preheat a griddle or another large skillet over medium heat and melt the butter. Crack the eggs onto the griddle and fry 3 to 4 minutes undisturbed for sunny-side up, or 2 to 3 minutes per side for over easy, or to your taste.

+ To serve, spoon the warm hash onto 4 individual plates, top the hash with a fried egg, and serve right away.

BEHIND THE NAME

Hang a few desperados and suddenly a town's got a reputation. That's what came of the central California city we know today as Placerville in the Sierra Nevada foothills, which earned the Hangtown nickname in the mid–nineteenth century. A couple of accounts of the Hangtown fry recipe's origins differ slightly but represent a common inspiration. One nodded to a convicted criminal wanting to burden the local coffers with his last meal request, the other credits a newly rich prospector wishing to flaunt his wealth. Either way it came down to the triad of eggs, bacon, and oysters, three of the most expensive ingredients for that time and place. They may be relatively less expensive today but the combination still tastes indulgent. With a little dose of history tossed in.

THIS IS A delightfully simple batter that takes moments to whip together—just flour, ale, and salt. There's pretty good flexibility relative to the beer you use, though I'd stay away from distinctly flavored beers like hoppy IPAs or dark stouts. The potato-frying method may sound odd, but it's inspired by one I picked up from the bright folks at Cook's Illustrated *and have used many times. There's no fussing about oil temperature or double-frying as is often recommended.*

ALE-BATTERED OYSTERS & CHIPS

MAKES 4 SERVINGS

Vegetable oil, for deep-frying

2 russet potatoes (about 1½ pounds), well scrubbed and dried

Kosher salt

FOR THE BATTER:

1½ cups unbleached all-purpose flour

1½ cups (12-ounce bottle) pale ale, plus more (or a splash of water) if needed

½ teaspoon kosher salt

24 freshly shucked medium to large oysters (see Shucking Oysters, page 31) or jarred small to medium oysters, drained

+ Preheat the oven to 200 degrees F. Line a rimmed baking sheet with brown paper or paper towels and set an oblong wire rack on top, if you have one.

+ Put a few inches of oil in a Dutch oven or other large, deep, heavy saucepan; it should come no more than halfway up the sides of the pan. Cut the potatoes lengthwise into ⅜-inch-thick slices, then cut those slices lengthwise into roughly ⅜-inch-wide strips. Add the potatoes to the oil and set the pan over medium-high heat. The oil will slowly come to a boil in about 7 to 10 minutes; gently stir occasionally with a wire skimmer or long-handled metal tongs during this time to ensure the potatoes aren't sticking to each other. When the oil is boiling, continue cooking the potatoes, stirring just very gently on occasion to avoid sticking, until the potatoes are evenly and well browned, 15 to 20 minutes longer. Carefully lift out and transfer the fries to one side of the prepared baking sheet, sprinkle lightly with salt, and set in the oven to keep them warm while frying the oysters.

(CONTINUED)

Fennel Tartar Sauce (page
  91) or store-bought,
  for serving

Lemon wedges, for serving

+ Adjust the heat under the pan if needed to arrive at about 350 degrees F (use a deep-fry or candy thermometer to check the temperature).

+ While the oil is adjusting, make the batter. In a medium bowl, combine the flour, ale, and salt, and whisk gently to mix. The batter should have the consistency of heavy cream; if it's too thick, add a bit more beer or water.

+ Dip 6 of the oysters into the batter, allowing excess to drip off, and slide them carefully into the oil. Fry until nicely brown, about 3 minutes. Transfer the oysters to the baking sheet with the fries and return the baking sheet to the oven. Continue coating and frying the remaining oysters, allowing the oil to reheat between batches as needed.

+ Arrange the fried oysters and potatoes on individual plates, add a generous dollop of tartar sauce alongside with lemon wedges, for squeezing, and serve right away.

STEAMED & POACHED

THIS STEW IS the essence of oysters and one of the most timeless ways of preparing them. Simple as it is, there are many variations, usually related to the liquid element: anything from just milk to full-on cream. In fact, old menus I've seen offered options for the diner, such as a milk stew for sixty cents or the richer cream version for seventy-five. I opt for hybrid here with half-and-half, though feel free to play around with the degree of creaminess to suit your taste.

OYSTER STEW

MAKES 4 TO 6 SERVINGS

6 tablespoons unsalted butter, divided

3 cups half-and-half

16 to 20 ounces jarred yearling or extra-small oysters, with their liquor

Kosher salt and freshly ground black pepper

Oyster Crackers (page 118) or store-bought, for serving

✦ Melt 4 tablespoons of the butter in a heavy-bottomed medium saucepan over medium heat. Warm the half-and-half in a small saucepan over medium-low heat. Cut the remaining 2 tablespoons butter into 4 to 6 even pieces and set aside.

✦ Add the oysters and their liquor to the melted butter. Cook, shaking the pan gently now and then, until the oysters have plumped a bit and their edges begin to curl, 2 to 3 minutes. Add the warm half-and-half with a small pinch each of salt and pepper. Cook over medium heat, stirring gently now and then, until hot, 2 to 3 minutes.

✦ To serve, ladle the stew into individual warmed shallow bowls. Top each stew with a piece of the reserved butter and another grinding of black pepper. Serve right away, with oyster crackers alongside for sprinkling over the stew.

EVERY ESCABECHE I'D ENCOUNTERED before seemed to have a lot going on: slivered vegetables, chiles, various seasonings in addition to the vinegar-heavy base. But while in Galicia in northwest Spain, I tasted the local mussels en escabeche and the dish was blessedly simple and outrageously delicious: olive oil, a touch of vinegar, paprika. It inspired this approach with oysters, which makes a wonderful appetizer or cocktail snack.

This is a recipe for which the spice's freshness is paramount, particularly a spice like paprika that is relatively mellow to begin with. This may be the perfect time to invest in some fresh paprika; I buy bulk spices in smaller portions that I'm likely to go through pretty quickly. In place of regular sweet paprika (which means "not spicy" in this case, as for "sweet" bell peppers), you can also use Spanish smoked paprika.

For marinating the oysters, choose a small, squat dish in which the oysters will be fully covered by the marinade, ideally one with a tight-fitting lid so you can just shake gently now and then to ensure even marinating.

OYSTERS EN ESCABECHE

MAKES 6 TO 8 SERVINGS

FOR THE MARINADE:

1 cup olive oil, plus more if needed

1 tablespoon sweet paprika (regular or smoked)

¼ cup red wine vinegar

1 bay leaf, preferably fresh, torn into 3 or 4 pieces

1 teaspoon kosher salt

✦ In a small saucepan over low heat, stir together the oil and paprika and warm for about 15 minutes to draw the paprika flavor into the oil. Take the pan from the heat and let it cool for 5 to 10 minutes, then stir in the vinegar, bay leaf, and salt. Set the marinade aside.

✦ If using in-shell oysters, steam them open (see note on page 123), 5 to 10 minutes. While still warm, but not too hot to handle, remove the oysters from the shells (some shells may not have fully opened, so you will need a shucking knife to help here) and add them to the marinade. Stir to be sure the marinade is evenly coating the oysters and set aside just until cooled to room temperature.

(CONTINUED)

+ If using jarred oysters, put the oysters and their liquor in a small saucepan and warm, stirring gently now and then, until the oysters plump up and their edges curl, 4 to 5 minutes. Set the pan aside for a few minutes to cool a bit, then lift the oysters from the pan with a slotted spoon and add them to the marinade. Stir to be sure the marinade is evenly coating the oysters and set aside just until cooled to room temperature.

+ Transfer the cooled oysters and marinade to a medium nonreactive container; the oysters should be fully submerged in the marinade; add a bit more oil if needed. Cover and refrigerate for at least 2 hours, or longer if the oysters are on the bigger side. The oysters can marinate for up to 3 days before serving. Stir now and then to reblend the seasonings and ensure even marinating.

+ To serve, allow the oysters to come to room temperature. Discard the bay leaf. Transfer the oysters to a serving dish, drizzle some of the marinade over, and serve with crackers or baguette alongside.

24 small oysters in their shells, shells well rinsed, or jarred yearling to extra-small oysters, with their liquor

Crackers or sliced baguette, for serving

FRESH BAY

Bay is rarely among the fresh herbs tucked into our window boxes or backyard gardens. But when I needed some fresh bay to test a recipe about twenty years ago, I bought a little four-inch pot of the herb, used what I needed for the recipe, and transplanted it to my patio garden. I still have that same bay—now a small tree—and can't tell you the last time I used a dried bay leaf. Dried bay has its place in stocks and stews, but fresh bay has a whole different character, with more vivid flavor that is almost reminiscent of nutmeg. Use it as you would dry bay, though it is versatile enough to even use in desserts.

THIS RECIPE USES BOTH the common form of celery we know well and the less common celery root, a rather gnarly looking ball that grows underground and has a subtle, earthy celery flavor. The root needs to be peeled with a knife rather than a vegetable peeler, as the skin is quite craggy in parts and thicker than you might think. First cut off the top and bottom of the root to expose the white flesh, then cut downward around the sides to remove the rest of the skin. Try to avoid cutting away too much of the white flesh.

A bisque is often enriched with cream, but you won't even miss the cream in this soup—it still tastes quite luxurious. For a little extra flavor, you could chop some smoked oysters and scatter a bit in the center of each serving along with the tender celery leaves. The soup is delicious too using half the amount of oysters, though the oyster flavor is quite subtle then.

OYSTER & CELERY ROOT BISQUE

MAKES 6 SERVINGS

3 tablespoons unsalted butter

2 cups finely chopped onion

2 cups finely chopped celery, preferably the tender interior stalks

¾ cup dry white wine

1 large or 2 small celery roots (about 1½ pounds), trimmed and diced

3 cups water, plus more if needed

✦ Melt the butter in a large saucepan over medium heat. Add the onion and celery stalks and cook, stirring often, until the vegetables begin to soften and turn translucent, 5 to 7 minutes. (They should not brown; reduce the heat if needed.) Add the wine and simmer over medium-high heat until the liquid has reduced by about half and the vapor no longer smells strongly of wine, 2 to 3 minutes.

✦ Add the celery root and water with a large pinch of salt and bring just to a boil over medium-high heat. There should be enough liquid so that the celery root floats a bit; add about ½ cup more water if needed. Reduce the heat to medium-low, cover the pan, and simmer until the celery root is very tender, 30 to 35 minutes. Add the oysters and their liquor and simmer until the oysters are plump and the edges have curled, 3 to 5 minutes.

+ Using an immersion blender, or by transferring the mixture in batches to a food processor or blender, puree the vegetables and oysters until very smooth. Reheat the bisque gently over medium-low heat. Season to taste with salt and pepper.

+ Pile the celery leaves on a cutting board and cut across them into shreds.

+ To serve, ladle the bisque into individual shallow warmed bowls and add a small mound of the celery leaves to the center, along with a drizzle of sherry. Serve right away.

Kosher salt

16 to 20 ounces jarred small to medium oysters, with their liquor

Freshly ground black pepper

About ½ cup loosely packed tender celery leaves

Dry sherry, for serving (optional)

OYSTER CRACKERS ARE easy enough to come by in the snack aisle of your grocery store. But with not too much effort, you can make a batch from scratch and add extra homemade panache to the Oyster Stew (page 112) or pretty much any soup. Heck, they make a great snack as is for cocktail hour.

OYSTER CRACKERS

MAKES ABOUT 4 CUPS CRACKERS, *enough for a couple dozen servings of soup, or snacking for 8 to 12 people*

2 cups unbleached all-purpose flour, plus more for kneading

1 teaspoon kosher salt

½ cup warm water (105 to 110 degrees F), plus more if needed

2 teaspoons (1 envelope) active dry yeast

⅓ cup unsalted butter, melted and slightly cooled

✦ In a medium bowl, stir together the flour and salt, then make a well in the center. Pour the warm water into the well and sprinkle the yeast over, stirring it gently into the water. Let the mixture sit until the yeast is frothy, about 5 minutes. Gently stir to start blending the wet and dry ingredients, drizzle the butter over, and continue stirring until a cohesive dough forms. If the dough is a bit dry, add another 1 to 2 tablespoons warm water. Knead the dough on the counter for a few minutes, with a little flour if the dough's sticky, until smooth and satiny. Put the dough back in the bowl, cover with a kitchen towel, and set aside in a warm place until doubled in bulk, about 1 hour.

✦ Preheat the oven to 375 degrees F. Line 2 baking sheets with parchment paper or silicone baking mats.

✦ Turn the dough out onto the counter, punch it down, and cut the dough in half. On a lightly floured work surface, roll out one half of the dough to a square about 7 by 7 inches with a thickness of about ¼ inch. With the rolling blade of a pizza cutter or plain (not fluted) pastry wheel, cut the dough into ½-inch strips in each direction, making ½-inch squares. Use a spatula to transfer sections of the squares to the baking sheet, then separate them so they don't touch while baking. Bake until the crackers are well puffed and lightly but evenly browned, 15 to 18 minutes. Some crackers around the edges of the baking sheet may be done sooner than those in the center; transfer them to a wire rack (or a plate, some racks may not have fine enough mesh to hold the crackers) to cool and continue baking the rest for a few minutes longer. Repeat with the remaining dough portion.

✦ When all the crackers have cooled, transfer some to a basket or bowl for serving, for guests to sprinkle over their own chowder or nibble. Store any remaining crackers in an airtight container for up to 1 week.

WHILE THE OYSTER STEW (page 112) is simplicity itself, this recipe isn't too many paces beyond that. Leeks and bacon bring earthy flavor and aroma to the mix, but the oysters still lead the charge in this simple, unthickened soup (not at all like a thick clam chowder). Feel free to scatter some oyster crackers over before serving if you like, maybe even your own homemade version (see page 118). You can skip the bacon, in which case you might want to use a bit more sliced leek and/or diced potato.

OYSTER CHOWDER

MAKES 4 TO 6 SERVINGS

3 strips thick-cut bacon, cut across into ¼-inch pieces

1 medium leek, trimmed and cleaned (see note on page 70), white and light-green parts thinly sliced

8 ounces Yukon Gold potatoes, scrubbed and cut into ¼-inch dice

3 cups half-and-half

16 to 20 ounces jarred yearling or extra-small oysters, with their liquor

Kosher salt and freshly ground black pepper

Minced fresh chives or flat-leaf parsley, for serving

Chive blossoms, for serving (optional)

+ Fry the bacon in a medium, heavy-bottomed saucepan over medium heat until aromatic and much of the fat has rendered, 3 to 5 minutes. (The bacon shouldn't brown much, reduce the heat if needed.) If there is more than a couple tablespoons of fat, pour off the excess (it can be saved for another use).

+ Add the leek to the pan and cook, stirring occasionally, until tender but not browned (as before, reduce the heat if needed to avoid browning), 3 to 5 minutes. Add the potatoes and half-and-half, bring just to a low boil, then reduce the heat to low, cover the pan, and simmer gently until the potatoes are tender, 10 to 12 minutes.

+ Add the oysters and their liquor and simmer, uncovered, over medium heat, stirring gently now and then, until the oysters are plump and their edges are curled, 3 to 4 minutes. Season the chowder to taste with salt and pepper.

+ To serve, ladle the chowder into individual warmed shallow bowls, sprinkle with the chives and chive blossoms, and serve right away.

THIS IS A French butter sauce with an Asian flavor, made by whisking chilled butter into reduced sake that's been spiked with fresh ginger. Spooned over simply steamed oysters, the results defy how easy it is to make.

STEAMED OYSTERS WITH SAKE-GINGER BUTTER SAUCE

MAKES 4 TO 6 APPETIZER SERVINGS

¾ cup dry sake

1 tablespoon finely grated peeled fresh ginger, plus more for serving

5 tablespoons unsalted butter, cut into 6 to 8 pieces and chilled

Kosher salt

12 small to medium oysters in their shells, shells well rinsed

✦ In a small saucepan, combine the sake and ginger and stir with a whisk to mix. Set the pan over medium-high heat and boil until reduced to about 2 tablespoons, 5 to 7 minutes. Reduce the heat to low and whisk in the butter, a couple pieces at a time, allowing each addition to melt creamily into the sauce before adding the next. When all the butter has been added, whisk in a good pinch of salt, then set aside. Avoid overheating the sauce or the butter may become oily; low heat is important.

✦ Steam the oysters (see note on following page), about 12 minutes.

✦ Gently rewarm the sauce over low heat for 1 to 2 minutes, whisking constantly.

✦ Remove the top shell from each oyster and loosen the lower adductor muscle if needed. Arrange the oysters in their bottom (cupped) shells on individual plates. Spoon the warm butter sauce over, top with a tiny dab of fresh grated ginger, and serve right away.

HOW TO STEAM OYSTERS

Put the oysters in a large pot, arranging them as evenly as you're able (they shouldn't be more than 2 oysters deep). Pour about 1 cup of water over, cover the pot, and set over medium-high heat. Within a few minutes of the water boiling, the oysters may begin to open. Use tongs to transfer them to a large bowl and cover them with a towel or aluminum foil to help keep them warm. Continue steaming the remaining oysters until all have opened, or according to the time indicated in the recipe, whichever comes first. If there are any remaining unopened oysters, let them cool until you can handle them easily and use a shucking knife to open them.

THE PRODUCTION OF hard ciders has grown quite a lot in recent years; you'll likely see a number of options available at the store. Avoid sweeter styles for this recipe, opting instead for a dry cider that will complement the oyster flavor best. Apples naturally contain malic acid, which has a characteristic slightly sour flavor that complements the oysters wonderfully. You might want to get enough of the cider to sip some alongside as well.

CIDER-POACHED OYSTERS ON TOAST

MAKES 6 SERVINGS

- ✦ In a medium saucepan over medium-high heat, combine the oysters and the hard cider. Bring just to a low boil, then reduce the heat to medium-low and simmer, gently stirring occasionally, until the oysters are plump and their edges curl, 3 to 4 minutes. Drain, reserving the oysters and the liquid separately and discarding any grit left behind in the bottom of the saucepan. Set the oysters aside. Measure 2 cups of the liquid, discarding any extra or adding more cider if needed.

- ✦ Rinse the saucepan, then melt the butter in it over medium heat. Add the apple and cook, stirring often, until partly tender, about 2 minutes. Sprinkle the flour over, stir to evenly blend with the butter, then continue to cook, stirring, for 2 minutes (it might get rather thick, which is okay). Stir in the

18 freshly shucked small to medium oysters (see Shucking Oysters, page 31) or jarred extra-small to small oysters, drained

2 cups hard apple cider, plus more if needed

3 tablespoons unsalted butter, plus more for buttering

¾ cup finely chopped crisp tart apple, skin on (such as Braeburn, Granny Smith, or Fuji)

3 tablespoons unbleached all-purpose flour

¼ cup heavy cream

(CONTINUED)

Kosher salt

6 slices (not too thick) country-style bread

About 3 tablespoons minced fresh chives, for serving

reserved poaching liquid and cook, stirring often, until thick enough to coat the back of the spoon, 3 to 4 minutes. Stir in the cream and season to taste with salt. Return the poached oysters to the sauce and warm gently over low heat for a few minutes.

✦ While the oysters are warming, toast the bread. Lightly butter the bread, then halve each piece diagonally. Set the toast pieces, slightly overlapping, in the center of individual plates. Spoon the oysters and sauce on the toast, scatter chives over, and serve right away.

OYSTER EXCURSIONS

Traveling at the insistence of our stomachs is nothing new. Food lovers often plot their weekend road trips and vacation getaways around specific foods they want to savor. Oyster lovers have a rich array of options, from visiting oyster beds and breathing in the sea air where the beloved bivalves thrive, to attending rowdy and rambunctious celebrations in honor of the oyster. These are just a sample of what you may want to put on your calendar or add to an upcoming vacation itinerary.

YEAR-ROUND (OR ALMOST)

Hog Island Oyster Farm

There are a number of options here at the Marshall, California, home base for Hog Island Oyster Co. You can buy oysters to take home, buy oysters to stay and shuck yourself (they provide the tools and a quick lesson), or hit The Boat, their outdoor café for shucked-to-order oysters, grilled oysters, and other items to round out your picnic (charcuterie, cheese, salads). Regular picnic tables are first-come, first-served, and those with grills can be booked ahead. Beverages are available too. Tours are offered a few days a week. And there's a taste of Hog Island at their San Francisco and Napa restaurants as well.

HogIslandOysters.com

Humboldt Bay Oyster Tours

Not too many tourism centers feature an oyster bar, but you can slurp a few while at Taste in the Humboldt Bay Tourism Center in Eureka, California. There are two oyster tours that you can book while there; both include a boat trip on the bay with educational input from a local oyster farmer and one includes bonus time on the farm to pick your own oysters. *HumboldtBayTourismCenter.com*

The Oyster Saloon at Hama Hama Oysters

In addition to the retail store open year-round at their farm on Hood Canal in Lilliwaup, Washington, Hama Hama also has the outdoor Oyster Saloon (hours vary seasonally) where they serve oysters grilled, raw, fried, and in po'boys, along with chowder and steamed clams. Wine, beer, and cider are available too.
HamaHamaOysters.com

Taylor Shellfish Farms

The Shelton, Washington, home base of Taylor Shellfish Farms in south Puget Sound has a retail store, as does the Samish Bay location to the north. On Samish Bay you'll also find a picturesque shoreside picnic area with tables and grills where you can shuck and cook your just-purchased oysters. For an urban Taylor Shellfish experience hit one of the three oyster bars they've opened in Seattle.
TaylorShellfishFarms.com

Westcott Bay Shellfish

This farm on beautiful San Juan Island in Washington was undergoing renovation and reconstruction as I finished this book. The new facilities are due to include a retail store where you can buy oysters, with picnic tables (and grills too down the line) to sit and enjoy them on the spot. *WestcottBayShellfish.com*

ANNUAL & SEASONAL EVENTS

Slurp

One Sunday in late April or early May, oyster lovers converge on Fish Tale Brew Pub in Olympia, Washington, where local oyster growers are on hand shucking their just-harvested oysters. There is also a celebrity slurp-off, Fish Tale beers and Washington wines, other seafood from local chefs, music, and other offerings. Proceeds support the Pacific Coast Shellfish Growers Association's Shellfish Habitat Restoration Fund. *PCSGA.org/slurp*

Hama Hama Oyster Rama

The date floats a bit, but they aim for some time in April or early May while it's still cool enough for oysters to be in prime form and (likely) warm enough for folks to want to gather for an outdoor party, with a low tide to offer access to the oyster beds. For the one-day gathering on Washington's Hood Canal, there are food booths, an oyster relay and other oyster-y games, live music, and a beer garden—but really, spending time on that beach and communing with the oysters is the heart and soul of the event.

HamaHamaOysters.com

Comox Harbour Charters

About once a month over the summer, Comox Harbour Charters offers their popular oyster tours, when they venture across Baynes Sound in British Columbia to visit the deep-water production of Hollie Wood Oysters. Guests learn about the oyster-growing operation in an incredibly beautiful setting and sample oysters on the way back to the dock, which are prepared by a guest chef who is along for the ride.

ComoxHarbourCharters.com

Arcata Bay Oyster Festival

In honor of the important oyster industry heritage on California's Humboldt Bay (within which Arcata Bay sits), this festival, held the Saturday before Father's Day each year, is a day packed with creative oyster fun. Among highlights are the Shuck and Swallow Contest, where teams of two vie to shuck and slurp the most oysters, and an oyster-calling contest (call it Humboldt quirky).

OysterFestival.net

Shelton OysterFest

The first weekend of October is blocked out for many Northwest oyster lovers, because there is nowhere else to be but in Shelton, Washington, for a two-day indulgence of oysters. There are cook-offs, food booths (the grilled oysters are always my favorite), and live entertainment. But here too are serious shucking competition heats that will take the weekend's top shucker to the national shucking competition at the St. Mary's County Oyster Festival in Maryland.

OysterFest.org

Oyster New Year

The first Saturday of November, Elliott's Oyster House hosts one of the biggest oyster parties Seattle sees each year. A few dozen oyster growers are on hand shucking their oysters at the seemingly-never-ending oyster bar—true bliss for the biggest among oyster fans. Many oyster-friendly beers and wines are poured, and there is an array of other foods, live music, and a "most beautiful oyster" contest, among other fun. It's all for a good cause too: proceeds go to the Puget Sound Restoration Fund.

ElliottsOysterHouse.com/ony

Clayoquot Oyster Festival

On the rustic and wonderful west coast of Vancouver Island, Tofino, British Columbia, puts on quite a party to celebrate local oysters the third week of November each year. The multiday event includes farm tours, a gala with oyster dishes from local chefs, and—an event I can't wait to attend myself—The Mermaid's Masquerade, a sea-themed costume ball with a bounty of oysters to slurp.

OysterGala.com

The Walrus & Carpenter Picnic

I'm not sure if there's a more unique and wonderful oyster excursion than this one, named for Lewis Carroll's oyster-escapade poem. The brainchild of oyster guru Jon Rowley in cooperation with Taylor Shellfish Farms, this is for devotees who don't mind an hour-plus bus ride from

Seattle to Totten Inlet on Washington's Puget Sound, at night, in the winter, in all weather. It was quite rainy the night I went, but I promise there were no dampened spirits! The trips always sell out. Tables along the shoreline feature just-shucked oysters and a few oyster-friendly wines to sip. Or, pick up an oyster from the beach, shuck it yourself, and slurp it down: pure magic. A bonfire's going both for warmth and for grilling a few oysters. And you'll get a reviving cup of oyster stew as well. There are just a few trips each winter—dates depend on convergence of time and tide so that the logistics work out.

RestorationFund.org/events/walrus

OYSTER RESOURCES

A FEW FAVORITE BOOKS

A Geography of Oysters
by Rowan Jacobsen (2007)

Subtitled "The Connoisseur's Guide to Oyster Eating in North America," this book covers an impressive range of territory relating to oysters. The coolest is Jacobsen's detailed discussion of specific oysters grown from Canada's Maritime provinces down around the Gulf Coast and up the Pacific coast to Alaska. Jacobsen is one well-traveled oyster lover.

Heaven on the Half Shell
by David G. Gordon, Nancy E. Blanton, and Terry Y. Nosho (2001)

This is a wonderful book that devotes a lot of attention to the foundation of the Northwest region's oyster industry, complete with many historic photos and illustrations. It helps paint a rich picture of why oysters matter so much in this area.

Consider the Oyster by Mary Frances Kennedy Fisher (1941)

This small and enchanting book is doubly magnificent because the topic is a beloved one to begin with, and it is studied through the prism of M. F. K. Fisher's wholly unique writing style that is enlightening, opinionated, poetic, inspiring, and funny all at once.

Meet Paris Oyster:
A Love Affair with the Perfect Food
by Mireille Guiliano (2014)

This story is woven in and around a tiny oyster bar in Paris, so it has a clearly Francophile perspective. But there is plenty of general discussion about the delights of eating oysters. And it will make sure you put Huitrerie Régis on a wish list for upcoming travel to France; I highly recommend it.

The Oyster Guide

This is the digital companion to Rowan Jacobsen's *A Geography of Oysters.*
OysterGuide.com

Oysterater

A newer web site recently launched by Rowan Jacobsen as a companion to his Oyster Guide, the Oysterater is a site where the oyster-loving community can learn about and rate a few hundred oysters, join forum discussions, and build your own personal list of favorites.
Oysterater.com

BC Oyster Guide

A great resource to learn more about oyster producers in British Columbia and the specific varieties they grow, along with a glossary of oyster terms and event listings. There's also an app version for download.
BCOysterGuide.ca

Willapa Bay Documentaries

Filmmaker Keith A. Cox and his team have produced a series of documentary videos highlighting Willapa Bay's oyster industry in the southwest corner of Washington State. You'll be able to view some videos directly on the website and others are available for purchase. Wonderful character comes through, with the interviews of many oyster growers and fascinating glimpses of the work they do.
StonyPix.com

In a Half Shell

Julie Qiu shares her ongoing exploration of oyster connoisseurship in this dynamic blog to help make enjoying oysters as easy as possible, even for the novice. Her focus has an east coast bent, but much of the information is general in nature and the Pacific Coast does get some attention. The blog includes shucking tips and more.
InAHalfShell.com

ORGANIZATIONS

Puget Sound Restoration Fund

Though their mission is about more than just oysters, the work of the PSRF supports many projects and activities related to oyster habitats and restoration. Among them are community shellfish farms, a means by which you can be directly involved in the process.

RestorationFund.org

Pacific Coast Shellfish Growers Association

PCSGA is a trade organization supporting the growers in the industry, but the site also includes consumer information about restoration initiatives, species, growers in the region, events, and more.

PCSGA.org

OYSTER SHOPPING GUIDE

Taylor Shellfish Farms

oysters both shucked and in-shell
TaylorShellfishStore.com

Hama Hama Oyster Company

oysters both shucked and in-shell
HamaHamaStore.com

Goose Point Oysters

oysters both shucked and in-shell
Store.GoosePoint.com

Ekone Oyster Company

smoked oysters
EkoneOyster.com

Mutual Fish Company

usually has eight to twelve or more varieties of oysters available at any time
MutualFish.com (for information only, orders placed by phone)

ACKNOWLEDGMENTS

Many folks in the oyster business were generous with their time and expertise, including Bill Taylor, Jeff Pearson, and "Oyster Bill" Whitbeck, among others at Taylor Shellfish Farms; Lissa James Monberg at Hama Hama Oyster Company; John Finger, Terry Sawyer, George Curth, and Brenna Schlagenhauf at Hog Island Oyster Co.; and Greg Dale at Coast Seafoods.

Margaret Pilaro Barrett, executive director of the Pacific Coast Shellfish Growers Association and Betsy Peabody, executive director of the Puget Sound Restoration Fund provided a wealth of information and perspective that I found invaluable. Many others working in or with the oyster industry contributed input as well, including Jerrod Davis, Director of the Office of Environmental Health & Safety, Washington State Department of Health; Roberta Stevenson, executive director of British Columbia Shellfish Growers Association; Alex Manderson, shellfish specialist with the Oregon Department of Agriculture Food Safety and Animal Health Program; and Laura Hoberecht, PhD, Aquaculture Coordinator for NOAA National Marine Fisheries Service.

I gained valuable insight about the biology of oysters and their role in our local ecology from Dr. Jennifer Ruesink, professor, University of Washington Department of Biology.

It was a pleasure to spend time talking with Portland chef Cory Schreiber to learn more about his family's role in Oregon's oyster history.

Many friends and colleagues lent me their taste buds and their opinions in the course of testing recipes, slurping oysters, and generally contemplating the most delicious ways to enjoy them. Particular thanks to

Susan Volland, Jake Kosseff, Kathy Casey, and Robert Hess. And to Cathy Sander and Vanessa Ruedebusch for help with testing recipes.

Huge thanks to the Hogensons for loaning me their cozy island home for the perfect writing retreat.

Thanks to Gary Luke at Sasquatch Books for the nudge to write this book; it has been a particularly wonderful and delicious adventure. And what a pleasure to work with such a talent as photographer Jim Henkens, who lent marvelous visual perspective to the story of Pacific Coast oysters.

And finally, special thanks to Jon Rowley, who I've known since I was a little spat of a food writer. I would not venture to guess how many oysters I've consumed in his presence. But sitting on top of that pile of discarded shells we'd have a nice view of the waters where oysters are such an important part of our Northwest seascape. As the inimitable R. W. Apple titled an article he wrote about Jon in the *New York Times*, "The Oyster is his World." And so many of us benefit from him sharing that oyster-loving world with us.

INDEX

NOTE: Photographs are indicated by *italics*.

Hama Hama Oysters,
The Oyster Saloon at, 128

Hangtown Hash with
Fried Eggs, *104*, 105–106

Hangtown nickname, origins of, 106

health benefits of oysters, 34

Hog Island Oyster Co., 13, 15, 23, 127

Hog Island Oyster Farm, 127

Hollie Wood Oysters, 130

Humboldt Bay Oyster Tours, 128

J

jarred oysters, 26, 28–29, 31

K

Kale Gratin with Brown-Butter
Crumbs, Oyster and, 75–77, *76*

keystone species, 4–5

Kimchi-Cucumber Relish, *62*, 63

Kumamoto oysters, *10*, 11–12

L

L & E Oyster Bar, 21, 23

leeks, tips for cleaning, 70

Leeks and Thyme, Baked Oysters
with Tender, *68*, 69–70

Lemon-Rosemary Mignonette, *54*, 55

Lopez Island Shellfish, 13, 15

M

meroir, x, 7

mignonettes
about, 50–51
Champagne Vinegar–Roasted
Shallot Mignonette, 53
Lemon-Rosemary
Mignonette, *54*, 55
Rice Vinegar–Ginger
Mignonette, 56

Moveable Feast, A (Hemingway), 37

O

ocean acidification, 17

off-bottom culture, 8

Okonomiyaki, Oyster, 96–97

Olympia oysters, *10*, 12

Oregon, xiii, 16, 20–21

Oregon Oyster Farms, xiii, 20

oyster bar culture, 19–23

oyster culture, ix–xiii

oyster excursions and events, 127–132

Oyster New Year, 131

oysters
beverages, pairing with, 35–41
buying, 25–27, 35, 135
cleaning, 28
growing regions of, 15–16
health and safety, 34–35

Smokey Tomato-Bacon Relish, 86

soups and stews

Oyster and Celery
Root Bisque, 116–117

Oyster Chowder, *120*, 121

Oyster Stew, 112

Spinach Puffs, Green
Curry Oyster and, 73–74

steamed and poached oysters, 111–126

steaming oysters, tips for, 123

Stew, Oyster, 112

storing oysters, 27–28

Swan Oyster Depot, 20, 21

T

Taylor Oyster Bars, 20, 21

Taylor Shellfish Farms, 13, 128,
131–132

Tequila Chaser,
Gazpacho Relish with, 65

Togarashi Slaw,
Oyster Sliders with, 93–95, *94*

Tomato-Bacon Relish, Smokey, 86

tumbled oysters, 8–9

W

Walrus and Carpenter
Picnic, The, 131–132

Walrus and the Carpenter, The, 21

Washington, 5, 12, 15, 21, 128–132

Westcott Bay Shellfish, 129

wine, pairing with oysters, 37, 39

CONVERSIONS

VOLUME

UNITED STATES	METRIC	IMPERIAL
¼ tsp.	1.25 ml	
½ tsp.	2.5 ml	
1 tsp.	5 ml	
½ Tbsp.	7.5 ml	
1 Tbsp.	15 ml	
⅛ c.	30 ml	1 fl. oz.
¼ c.	60 ml	2 fl. oz.
⅓ c.	80 ml	2.5 fl. oz.
½ c.	125 ml	4 fl. oz.
1 c.	250 ml	8 fl. oz.
2 c. (1 pt.)	500 ml	16 fl. oz.
1 qt.	1 l	32 fl. oz.

LENGTH

UNITED STATES	METRIC
⅛ in.	3 mm
¼ in.	6 mm
½ in.	1.25 cm
1 in.	2.5 cm
1 ft.	30 cm

WEIGHT

AVOIRDUPOIS	METRIC
¼ oz.	7 g
½ oz.	15 g
1 oz.	30 g
2 oz.	60 g
3 oz.	90 g
4 oz.	115 g
5 oz.	150 g
6 oz.	175 g
7 oz.	200 g
8 oz. (½ lb.)	225 g
9 oz.	250 g
10 oz.	300 g
11 oz.	325 g
12 oz.	350 g
13 oz.	375 g
14 oz.	400 g
15 oz.	425 g
16 oz. (1 lb.)	450 g
1½ lb.	750 g
2 lb.	900 g
2¼ lb.	1 kg
3 lb.	1.4 kg
4 lb.	1.8 kg

TEMPERATURE

OVEN MARK	FAHRENHEIT	CELSIUS	GAS
Very cool	250–275	130–140	½–1
Cool	300	150	2
Warm	325	165	3
Moderate	350	175	4
Moderately hot	375	190	5
	400	200	6
Hot	425	220	7
	450	230	8
Very Hot	475	245	9

ABOUT THE AUTHOR

CYNTHIA NIMS is a lifelong Northwesterner who reveled in growing up surrounded by great food—both in her mother's kitchen and exploring the region with her family, whether eating grilled oysters on a San Juan Island beach or huckleberry pancakes while backpacking in the Olympic Mountains. After graduating from the University of Puget Sound, having majored in mathematics and French literature, Cynthia followed her dreams and went to France to study cooking at La Varenne Ecole de Cuisine. There, she received the Grand Diplôme d'Etudes Culinaires and worked on numerous cookbooks with the school's president, Anne Willan, including *Great Cooks and Their Recipes* and ten in the Look & Cook series.

Cynthia is the author of over a dozen cookbooks. Her latest cookbooks were produced on Kindle, including *Crab*, *Wild Mushrooms*, *Salmon*, and four other titles in the Northwest Cookbooks series. Her latest print cookbook, *Salty Snacks*, was released in 2012. She was also among the team of writers and editors for the groundbreaking Modernist Cuisine volumes released in 2011 and served as a writer for *The Photography of Modernist Cuisine* released in 2013.

Previously the editor of *Simply Seafood* magazine and food editor of *Seattle Magazine*, she has since been a contributor to *Cooking Light*, *Coastal Living*, *Alaska Airlines Magazine*, *Sunset*, and other magazines. She is an active member of the International Association of Culinary Professionals (having served as president of the board) and Les Dames d'Escoffier. Her blog, *Mon Appétit*, can be found at MonAppetit.com. Cynthia and her husband live in Seattle, WA.